Our Travels with Our Children to India

Abdul Khaliq Kaifi

Our Travels with Our Children to India

Bibliographical Information of the Deutsche Nationalbibliothek
This publication is listed in the Deutsche Nationalbibliographie of the Deutsche Nationalbibliothek; detailed bibliographical information can be accessed under http://dnb.d-nb.de

Printing, Production and Layout: BoD - Books on Demand, Norderstedt
ISBN: 978-3-7543-6445-1

Our Travels with Our Children to India

(This is a free translation of my previous work: "Unsere Reisen mit unseren Kindern nach Indien" from German into English which has been a little modified at some places.)

To fulfill the desire of my grandson Luis, I wrote my biography, and this motivated me to write about my travels to India, undertaken by me some thirteen times between the years of 1974 and 2016 together with my wife Maria, my daughters Tara and Ina and my son Jussi, and sometime later with our grandchildren Lilia, Matilda, Dina, Luis and Adrian. These travels narrate the reminiscences of my bygone days and the experiences and events of those times. We all remember so well our sojourns in India and wish to be there again and again.

1974 In this year began our first travel to India with my wife Maria and my daughters Tara (six years old) and Ina (three). At that time, a flight to a Third World country like India was not common and easy. Therefore, we had to take a train first from Bremen to Osnabruck (Germany) and from there to Amsterdam (Holland). Amsterdam was then the gathering point for overseas travels. In those days, flying was considered as luxurious, full of adventures and excitements. The greetings of the stewardess, exotic food served with silver cutlery, welcome drinks, the prompt services of air staff, and the joyful sight of travelers from different countries gave a unique flair of enjoyment. I think we were also on board of a long-distance plane for the first time. I only remember that we enjoyed the journey to Delhi. As soon as we left the airport, it was for the first time that Maria, Tara, and Ina saw so many people and so much poverty on the road as well as cows, goats, sheep, and dogs roaming freely over there. The rickshaws, taxis, camels, and elephants were waiting for customers. As recommended by a friend, we arrived at the Hotel Vikram in Lala Lajpat Nagar, which was supposed to have a swimming pool. Tara and Ina rushed to the pool but came back terrified, as they had seen some frogs jumping into the pool. At that time, Delhi was hardly developed and looked like a bureaucratic town. It was built as a new capital in 1931 by Edward Lutyens (1869 - 1944), where their administrative buildings and residences were constructed. Most of the Indians lived in old Delhi (purani Delhi), built by the Moghul emperor Shah Jahan (1592-1666). At dawn, Delhi became dark, calm, and deserted. We had difficulties finding a taxi or a rickshaw from Connaught Place to our hotel Vikram, some 4 kilometers (km) away. Mr. Gupta, a book publisher from Delhi whom I had met at the Frankfurt Book Fair in 1972, took us in his car to the places worth seeing. He arranged for us to visit a dancing ceremony of a girls' school in Daryaganj (purani Delhi), which was performed by the pupils wearing Indian costumes and dancing to Indian music. Tara and Ina were so much pleased to see it and to be among the small school children of India.

After a short stay in Delhi, we traveled to Agra on a state tourist bus with a guide. We left very early in the morning to cover the distance of 220 km to Agra. When we reached Mathura, some 160 km away from Delhi, most of us rested or were sleeping, but our guide woke up suddenly and said loudly: We are now passing the holy city of Mathura on the bank of the Yamuna, where God Krishna was born and lived with his beloved Radha and girl friends (Gopis). After this announcement, he dropped off to sleep again till we reached Agra. We visited the Taj Mahal, built by Shah Jahan for his beloved wife Mumtaz Mahal (1593–1631), the most visited mausoleum in the world. At the time of our visit, Agra looked like a rural place in every respect. We saw animals grazing and carts moving around the Taj. After the guide had shown us the Taj, he sent us to the shops of handicrafts and artifacts, where he surely received his share of the profits from. On our way back to Delhi, we visited Sekunderabad, 10 km away from the Taj, where the massive tomb of Akbar the Great (1556–1605) is situated. There a horde of well-fed monkeys followed the visitors and snatched food stuff from them. Tara and Ina remained close to us to avoid the touch of the monkeys. Due to the shortage of time, we did not go to the ruined city of Fatehpur Sikri, where Akbar the Great had lived for some time, debated with the religious heads of Hindus, Muslims, and Christians, and founded a universal religion (din ilahi) there. We returned to Delhi late in the night.

From Delhi, we traveled to Jaipur, the capital of Rajasthan, located 288 km away from Delhi and founded in1728 by Maharaja Jai Singh. Ina had lost one of her shoes somewhere in the train, so after reaching Jaipur, we first took a Rickshaw to buy a pair of shoes for her. Then we went to a hotel which had been recommended to us by the tourist office at the Jaipur Station. The hotel belonged to a British lady, a widow of one of the Maharajas of Jaipur. Unfortunately, we do not remember anymore the name of that beautiful hotel, surrounded by small cottages for the guests. But we do remember a tree in the courtyard of this hotel that was full of singing colorful birds and parrots typical of Rajasthan. Our children became so much fascinated by the presence and sounds of the birds that they listened to them for hours. We visited the palaces and residences (hawelis) of the Maharajas, the Wind Palace (hawa mahal), known for its windows (jharoka) for the Maharanis to see from outside. After sightseeing, we went shopping for handmade things. Maria bought some Rajasthani wooden figures from a farmer on the street; one of them is still now in our home in Bremen. After our return to Delhi, we took a train to my home in Shakra, as there were no direct trains from Jaipur to the state of Bihar then.

We reserved a compartment of our own for that journey of 1200 km to my place. In comparison to other villages, my village was better developed. It had a middle and a high school, a railway station (Dholi), a post office (daakghar),a police station (thana), a registry office (kachehri), a bazaar, and a haat (grain and vegetable market) in the evening. All that because of a British family who had a big farm in Dholi near our village on the bank of a river of burih Gandak (an old arm of the Ganges). The journey to our railway station in Dholi required more than two days of the journey from Delhi. There were only coal engines at that time, the railways ran on narrow gauges and had one-way lanes. Due to the lack of bridges and construction work for broader lanes, the trains took longer routes and more time. But we were in no hurry and had sufficient space for us in our compartment to relax and sleep in our up and down beds. We enjoyed the passing landscape, the coming and going of the passengers at the stations and the sellers of foodstuffs in our compartment and on doorways. On the whole, we arrived well in Shakra and our old house was still there, which was built in 1934 after the great earthquake with a scale of 8,4 in North Bihar and South Nepal. I was welcomed like a lost son with my new family members. I had not been there for some 12 years. Very soon, Maria, Tara, and Ina were surrounded by my family and our village inhabitants, who had never seen such faces before. My family was well prepared for us; the house was white washed, well cleaned, an electric fan hung in our sleeping room, and an anti-septic toilet was ready to use. But we soon noticed that electricity seldom functioned and only at awkward times when we were sleeping. So, we used the kerosene lamps for lighting and the stove to boil the water for drinking and washing. The food was prepared on a clay stove (chula), usually by a eunuch (hijra, mauga) and a deaf and dumb woman (bathia). Before the final settlement of the marriage our eunuch was often sent by us and other landed gentry to visit secretely the bride to check her body. Our house maids had no names, and no one knew where they came from.

Our relatives from nearby villages visited us and brought us the local specialty, a cackling hen or a duck. But they also came to peep into our room to see Maria in the permanent state of smoking and drinking whisky, a widely prevalent opinion of a white woman, the so-called Memsaheb, shared by the Indians. My maternal grandmother who, after the death of her only son, patronized me as her son was extremely happy to see me with my wife and my children. To keep the children busy with events, she let a tree climber (pasi) come to pluck down a coconut from a palm tree and presented the coconut milk to the children. She showed the children how to make green bananas ripe by keeping them underground and heating them from outside. Every day she arranged for the delivery of toast bread and cake from the city of Muzaffarpur (District town), 20 km away from Shakra, which were still made there by an old baker, who used to work earlier for the British. To show Maria, Tara, and Ina a traveling theatre (natak), a snake charmer (sapera), a dancing bear (bhalu), and the marriage of monkeys (Bandar ki biah) before our house were arranged. The children rode a buffalo or a pony, played with goats and discussed among them, who had the best goat. The children kept themselves busy for some hours by building a heap of rice and wheat on the veranda of our house and selling the pile among themselves. Tara once came to Maria in a hurry and reported to her mother that she had seen her grandmother spitting blood out of her mouth. On our inquiry, we came to know that she chewed betel nuts (paan) and spit out the red stuff into the pot. To her big surprise, Maria saw my grandmother once drawing a swastika (Hakenkreuz) with her finger on a heap of the newly harvested rice. She told us that she always marked them with a swastika as a sign of good harvest and good luck. Late at night, a watchman (chaukidar) always came to warn the villagers in a loud voice to remain vigilant of the thieves. Maria enjoyed the melodious shouting of the chowkidar. Next time, when I came to Shakra, the watchman was no more there, the system of the watchman had been abolished. One of my aunts whispered to me that a wizard (jaduwala) was going around our house every night with his spiritual stick and slogans (mantra, jhar phuk) to ban the evil spirits (jin, bhut). I have been accustomed to such practices since my childhood in India. I remember that once a lady of a very rich family in Delhi, had asked me to bring a witch from my village to get rid of a lower caste girlfriend of her son, who had fallen in love with her.

We came to know that a few weeks ago, a bus service for the first time had started from Muzaffarpur to Kathmandu (Nepal). Therefore we took the opportunity to visit Kathmandu, 400 km away. We left for Kathmandu by bus without exactly knowing the hazardous route and that it would take two days and two nights to get there. Our bus passed the area of Janakpur, the birthplace of Sita, the wife of Prince Rama from Ayodhya. She was abducted by the devil king Ravana from Sri Lanka. After a long fight with Rama together with his brother Laxman and the Hanumans (monkeys) she was rescued from Ravana, told in the most popular Indian epic of Ramayana. The first night of our journey, we had to stay in Birganj at the border of Nepal, where we could only find a very miserable hotel, full of dirt and mosquitoes, which we still remember as a mosquito hotel. Maria and I could not sleep there at all, but the children soon fell asleep. On the hilly way to Kathmandu, one of the passengers fell down from the bus in the middle of the night, but the driver did not stop the bus. A fellow traveler spoke to the driver and us about this, Maria prompted vehemently to stop the bus and to bring the man back. Ultimately, the lost passenger was brought back. I remember that Tara and Ina remained brave on the serpentine roads and enjoyed the mountainous panorama, which they had never seen before. In those days, there was hardly any plane service, tourism, and standard hotels in Kathmandu or elsewhere in India. However, we could find a reasonable hotel there, called Crystal with electric light, bed tea in the early morning and breakfast. In the city, we saw some very young hippies with children, who were arriving on trucks, playing the guitar, and as helpers to the Indian drivers. They were seen to live simply in make-shift camps, tents and seemed happy with music, meditation, and marihuana. Unfortunately, we had to vacate our hotel after two nights, as it had been booked in advance by another guest. So we changed, to a moderate hotel. Tara did not like the new abode. She snatched her small suitcase and went out of the room for the Crystal hotel. This abrupt response and protest of a then six-year-old girl was observed by the owner of our new hotel, who promised Tara to do all the best to make her stay a pleasant one. During our stay, we visited the palaces of the Ranas, temples, pagodas, and the Bhagmati river, where the Buddhists and Hindus worship and have their cremation ceremonies. Early in the morning, we went by bus to take a look at Mount Everest and saw a little bit of it. To avoid the long tiresome bus service from Kathmandu, we decided to fly with a propeller machine, and such air flights had also just started from Kathmandu to Bihar. The flight took only half an hour of the time till Raxaul (Bihar). After a very short stay in Shakra, we left the place for Bombay (now Mumbai). At the time of our departure, the whole village gathered at our house to say good- bye. My parents and relatives wept and thought that they would never see us again. Maria also felt very much touched by the affection and hospitality given to her and her children, and the tears came out of her eyes.

So, with broken hearts, we took a train for Benares (now called as Varanasi/Kashi). Candles were given to us for lighting our compartment at night. We covered the distance of 240 km in some 12 hours, reached Varanasi, and stayed there for a night in a retiring room of the station, built very elegantly by the British for the stay of their officers. After some search, we could find a private taxi and go to Sarnath, 10 km from Varanasi, where Gautama Buddha (563–483 B.C.) had preached his first sermon. The place is famous for its stone pillar, surmounted by the famous lion capital built by emperor Ashoka (273–232 B.C.), which has been adopted by the Government of India as its emblem. After visiting Sarnath, we went to the holy side of the Ganges in Varanasi, the most sacred river of the Hindus with its banks (ghats), famous for praying (puja), bathing (ashnan), and the burning of corpses (marghat). We walked to the streets (galis), where garments and silk clothes are sold, woven and embroidered (zaribooti) for centuries. Maria selected some clothes for the children and friends in Germany. After staying in Varanasi overnight, we took the train to Mumbai, which took two days and two nights for nearly 1480 km. We had once again booked a whole compartment for us for this long journey. At night we slept in our beds, and during the day, we played games with the children, watched the passengers at the stops with their bags, beddings, utensils, and listened to the shouts of the vendors (walas) of tea (chai), Indian cigarettes (biri), betel (paan), tobacco to sneeze (khini), peanuts (chinia badam), bananas (kela), guavas (amrood), puri (bread with mashed potatoes), pakoras, samosas, etc. We even saw herbal sellers (jaributiwala), blind musicians with sarangis, sadhus und fakirs, singing bhajans, kirtans (religious songs), and the mystic dohas (lines) of unity from Kabir in the Hindi dialect of Awadhi and Bhojpuri. On trains, one sees and meets the real India, its people in unique appearances, languages, and dialects. Many writers believe that Mahatma Gandhi (1869-1948) could not have achieved the freedom of India without his travels on the railways. After this long journey, we reached Mumbai in a good mood. We stayed in the hotel Chateau at Churchgate, which was run by a British lady, where we were served a British breakfast with egg and ham. On our first journey in 1974, we came across British men and women in India who had been living there for a long time and were too old to go back to Great Britain. The next time on our trip to India in 1978, we saw none of them anymore. In Mumbai, I first showed Maria, Tara and Ina my missionary college Wilson at Chowpatty, where I had studied from 1952 to 1956 for my Bachelor of Arts (B.A.) and Haji Ali in Worli, where I had lived with my parents for some time on a small island in the Arabic Sea. We also visited the famous station of Victoria Terminal, Crawford Market, Flora Fountain, and Colaba Market. We took our children to the Taraporewala Fish Aquarium at Marine Drive, the first of its kind in India. I went to meet Yahya Jasdanwala, an intimate friend of my deceased father in his insurance office at Flora Fountain, the industrialist and the agent of the British Petroleum Company in India, who after my graduation 1956 Mumbai arranged a job for me as a bookkeeper in the Petroleum Company of Qatar (Golf). He was so much pleased to see me with my wife and children and presented me as a success to his brothers there. He talked with Maria about his visit to Germany in the time of Nazi rule and his German Jockey for his horses in Mumbai and Poona.

Sadly we had to depart for Germany. With the exception of the bites of mosquitoes and other insects, we remained to save from tropical diseases in India all the time. This was due to all the medical measures taken by Maria in Germany and her hygienic pre-cautions in India. Another reason might have been that European children of those days were not so much accustomed to the luxurious living of these days.

1978 We traveled again to India and this time with three children. Jussi was three then, Tara ten, and Ina seven years old. We flew with Air India to Delhi via Moscow. I suppose Air India took this way to buy cheap petrol in Moscow. During the flight to Russia, it was announced that due to heavy snowfall in Moscow, our plane would be redirected towards Helsinki. Thus, we landed there late at night and were not allowed to leave the plane. After a wait of several hours in Helsinki, our plane started for Moscow, where we were directed to a shabby waiting room and had to remain there in silence without any provision of refreshments. An employee of Air India whispered to us not to be loud as talks were being bugged by the Russian secret service. Our good Indian food for the night was taken away by the Russian employees. Ultimately, we got a piece of hot dog, some boiled potatoes, and a drink. A packet of medicine, which we had handed over in Moscow to be kept in cold storage, was not given back to us. The unfriendly attitude of the staff and the atmosphare there left some unpleasant memories on us.

After this unexpected stay in Helsenki and Moscow, we arrived in Delhi some 18 hours late. This time we stayed in Safdar Jang with an old friend of mine, Yogesh, a bag pack traveler, who once lived with me in Cologne on his way to North Europe. Once, we witnessed a gathering in a park (maidan) with people shouting slogans of praise for long life (zindabad) and curses of death (mordabad) directed for an opponent. On my asking, I was told by Yogesh that these rural people had been hired by a politician for his election and had been brought here even from the nearby states of Haryana and Uttar Pradesh. For these hired people, it was a chance to see Delhi. As a matter of fact, they did not know him and his party. They should better hurry now to catch the busses for the return to their places; otherwise, they would be left in Delhi stranded. He added that in Delhi, eunuchs were hired to lament and beat chests at the funeral of a lonely rich man. After the integration of some 350 princely states by the Home Minister Sardar Vallabhai Patel (1875 – 1950) in 1950, a lot of eunchs for living migrated in the city of Delhi. During our stay, we wanted to finish up with the second injection of cholera for Jussi, the first one had already been given in Bremen. A doctor near our place gave him the injection, but after a few hours, he got some fever and his upper thigh swelled. Perhaps the doctor had used his own contaminated syringe instead of ours, given to him for this purpose. We became very worried, but thanks to God, the pain and swelling vanished the next day and he was fit again for our journey to Shakra. We did not stay long in Shakra, as my grandmother (nani) was no more alive and some close relatives had also died in between. After a short stay there, we left by train for Darjeeling via Siliguri, 400 km away. After a night of travel to Siliguri, we waited in the morning for the Toy Train to Darjeeling. While waiting on the platform, the children observed the crows fetching the biscuits from our bag and eating them right there. The daring invasion of those birds impressed the children, who were surprised and laughed at the happening. Darjeeling is only 88 km away from Siliguri and the Toy Train with its only two little compartments, ran on a track of 610 mm. The route having altogether 554 bridges with only one tunnel, was constructed by the British between 1879 and 1881.Due to the very slow speed of the train, the trip took eight hours. At one of the stops, I got off to buy something, but the train left the station without me. Maria and the children shouted because of my absence, the driver heard them and drove back to my waiting spot so that I could join my family happily and we all quenched our thirst with the pineapple juice, I had bought at the stop. We reached the hill station Darjeeling, located 2,200 meters (m) high above sea level. There we saw only Sherpa women working as coolies, who carried our bags and brought us to a hotel, which had been recommended by the station master of Darjeeling. After the independence of India in 1947, most of the British people left the hill resort. Their residences were largely converted into hotels. Although our room was big enough for sitting and sleeping, we slept together in one bed to keep ourselves warm. The owner provided us with hot water in containers, lamps for the night, and some breakfast in the morning. We saw a lot of hippies in Darjeeling living in camps, tents, abandoned houses, and on the street. We saw notes on entrances of restaurants to keep away the hippies, as "no hot water and hot soup available today". We visited the old residences, churches, convents, gardens, and cemeteries. At the time of our visit, Darjeeling was not a proper place for an Indian tourist. The British came here to enjoy the cool. Indians avoid chilly areas. On our short walks, we automatically came to know much of the city, and our children became acquainted with the area and shopkeepers. Once Tara and Ina wanted to go to the marketing without us, we allowed them for that but followed them behind. As soon as the bazaaris (shopkeepers) saw us, they showed us without our asking the going direction of our children, showing awareness of their responsibility to keep an eye on the children. Once Maria went with the children to an old cinema of the British days but came out soon as the lavatory had been out of use for a long time. We remember a request of Jussi, who was still sucking his thumb at that time, which had been crushed somewhere on the train, and asked Maria to request Ina for to put his thumb into her mouth. After having seen of Darjeeling, we left the place with teas and handmade woolen products of the refugees from Tibet. Instead of taking the Toy Train, we took a taxi to Siliguri and arrived there in less than two hours. So, we could see from near the Himalayan orchids, rhododendrons, tea plantations, and aboriginal women (adhivasi), engaged in plucking the tea leaves. In Siliguri, we took the train for Patna, about 400 km away. Patna is the capital of the province Bihar. In ancient times it was called Patliputra. The Mughals named it Azimabad and the British shortened it from Patliputra to Patna. The East India Company won the city in 1757 in the battle of Plassey (Bengal). My sister Gurya lived there with her family, her husband working there as a teacher in an American missionary school. From Siliguri, we had to cross the Ganges in Hajipur for Patna on a steamer. The Ganges is very broad there, and the water level was very uneven. So it took a zigzag course in search of deep water. The old steamer from British days was overloaded with passengers, agricultural products, and small animals for the city. Therefore we often had to shift, either to the left or to the right, to balance the weight of the steamer. We had the dreadful feeling of sinking somewhere in the Ganges. From Hajipur, you can see Patna with bare eyes, but it took at least hours to reach the terminal harbor (Digha Ghat) of Patna. After a search in the late evening, we could find a small hotel in a residential area of Patna. The city offers little from the earlier times to visit. Patliputra was the capital of the Maurya dynasty, where emperor Ashoka (273–232 B.C.) resided, and the city was once visited by Megasthenes (350–290 B.C.) as an ambassador of Selekus I, a diadochi of Alexander the Great (356–323 B.C.).

There is nothing left of it now. The capital is now lost in the water and the mud of the Ganges. We saw some interesting places of the Victorian age: the governor house, the high court, the secretariat, and the only ladies college in Bihar. A very interesting place to see is Azimabad from the days of Muslim rule, now old Patna city. Here exist the ruined havelis, the Khuda Baksh library with Islamic manuscripts, old British colleges, and the busiest Patna market, where Maria bought glass bracelets, necklaces, earrings, and some other typical Bihari ornaments for the children. During a sightseeing tour on a coach drawn by two horses (baggi), we saw Victorian buildings and a seller of birds (chiriawala), selling birds from all parts of India and the children insisted on buying some of them. We could, however, stop them from buying due to export restrictions and the difficulty of keeping the birds with us till our departure from India. The children enjoyed the hospitality of my sister and other relatives who had recently settled down in Patna.

After a few days, we left Patna for Mumbai, a distance of 1,450 km. A short while ago, the Indian railway had introduced a system of sleeping berths for long-distance travel, which was called Janta Express (common fast train). The former British railway system of 1st, 2nd, 3rd, and Inter-Class had been abolished. Therefore we could not book a separate compartment for us. Thus, we had the possibility now to travel with the masses and an opportunity to mix and talk with fellow passengers. We left Patna at night and went to sleep on our allocated wooden benches. I asked the persons sitting nearby to keep an eye on our trunks in the night. As we got up in the morning at Mughal Sarai station, we missed one of our trunks. While we were searching, a fellow passenger told us that the people whom I had trusted had left the train with a trunk in Buxar. Thank God, this stolen trunk only had dirty clothes in it, and we were all glad that our trunk with more expensive things and presents had not been taken away. On this occasion, I told Maria and the children about the place of Buxar where my grandfather was put in prison as a freedom fighter with Rajendra Prasad, the first president of free India (1950–1962). During our journey, we saw a peasant with his wife and two children in an aisle of the train busy cooking on a stove. He told us of his destination, which I knew was in the opposite direction. Maria became very upset at the mistake of the farmer and told me to tell him to get off at the next station. When I asked him to do that, he told me: Saheb, I have now just finished with my cooking. We shall eat first and sleep till morning, and then we shall get out somewhere and take a train in the opposite direction. Maria was very disappointed with the decision of this farmer. At that moment, I thought of Maria and her European way of thinking. And I thought of Rudyard Kipling (1865-1936), the author of "The Jungle Book", who saw enough of India and who once said: East is East, West is West and they will never come together. Surprisingly, none of the passengers in the train stopped the farmer from cooking. Even the conductor did not ask for the ticket or prohibited the farmer to cook in the aisle. This way of Indian thinking kept me engaged till we reached Mumbai. In Mumbai, my friend Prakash from Wilson college, arranged for our stay in the Automobile Club of India at Malabar hill. Near to this club, the Kamala Nehru Park is situated with its beautiful garden and playing facilities for the children. Prakash wanted to show us the city in his car, but the children preferred the double-deck bus. So, we took the bus to show the children again my college at Chowpatty and my earlier residence at Haji Ali. Although Mumbai is located on the coast of the Arabian See, there is hardly any sandy beach to be seen. The houses, hotels, shops, and markets had been constructed on the former beaches. Therefore, Prakash drove us some 12 km away from our club to a real beach in Juhu in Santa Cruz near the airport. As Jussi had swum in our Automobile Club before we left, he vomited during the drive. After everything had been in order again, we drove on to Juhu beach where we did a lot of sightseeing and had fun. During my period of study, 1952–1956, the place had only had some lonely settlements, but now I saw huge construction sites of skyscrapers, villas, and shopping malls. Our stay in Mumbai was made very pleasant by a friend called Ghadialiwala (trader of watches). He took us with his family to the Victoria Garden, where we made a picnic together, and the children rode on an elephant. He invited us to his Gujarati club at Marine Drive, where the Gujarati men and women had a country dance with local costume and with clubs and drums. Every evening, an old friend from my college days, Fakhru, brought grapes and apples for the children from Crawford market to our club in Malabar hill, some 10 km away. During my study in Mumbai, I taught his son reading and writing in English. As we waited at the airport in Santa Cruz for our return flight to Germany, some refreshments, as well as some cheese and bread, were served to us by Air India. When Ina saw the cheese, she cried with joy: Oh! wie lecker! (Oh, what a tasty!) The passengers sitting around us smiled and enjoyed the expression of the little girl. During her stay in India, Ina had always longed for German cheese. Meanwhile, some 40 years have gone by, but Maria and I remember even today such moving episodes with our children in India.

1993 After fifteen years, we went together again to India. Now the children were grown up and the daughters did not live with us anymore. Tara was studying medicine in Aachen, Ina journalism in Hamburg, and Jussi was preparing for his Abitur in Bremen. Meanwhile, the children were making their own holidays and went on educational exchanges and holiday trips with friends to foreign countries. But they showed eagerness to travel together with us to India to see the relatives, the village, the landscape, and the people there after such a long time. Maria, Jussi, and I first flew to Kolkata, where, after two days, Tara and Ina should join us. We reached the airport of Kolkata at 2.00 a.m. We were warned not to leave the airport at night due to the darkness and the thieves. Accordingly, we waited for the daylight and then took a taxi to our hotel in Lower Circular Road, about 15 km away from the airfield. Traveling in an old rattling taxi with broken doors, windows nearly demolished and seats very much broken and a driver half-drunken, made us extremely fearful, but Jussi being a young boy admired and enjoyed the zig-zag run of the car, the prompt reactions of the driver, who spat paan juice out of the window, horning at random, driving close to the still sleeping people on the foot paths and roaming animals. In spite of all of this, we reached our destination safely. Tara and Ina also reached Kolkata via Mumbai. They had not known why their plane had flown via Mumbai instead of Delhi to Kolkata, and they received a free stay and food in the magnificent hotel of Taj Mahal in Mumbai as compensation for the delay and the long journey. As arranged, we met them in our hotel in Lower Circular Road. The city of Kolkata lies on the river Hugli, an arm of the Ganges. The British East India Company came here first in 1690 and founded the city, kept it as its capital till 1931, ruled the British Empire in Asia and Africa from here. Independently from us, Tara and Ina often went to the city. Maria, Jussi, and I went together to see the Town Hall, the General Post Office, and the Howrah Station. We visited the Writers Building, which was built in 1777 by the East India Company, for the collection and writing of the taxes. In this building, we were received by a relative of mine, Ansar, from my village Shakra, who worked there in the city's planning department and showed us the historical parts of the building. Together we all made a city tour with a state bus to Dalhousie Square, Chowranghee Road, Queen Victoria (1819–1910) Memorial, and the Kali Temple of the angry goddess with her long tongue and four arms. One day, Maria, Jussi, and I went to the Howrah Boonton bridge. The bridge was constructed by the British in 1943. Being 705 m long, it was at that time the sixth-longest bridge in the world. From there, we decided to use a shuttle boat to go to the other side of the Howrah station. When the shuttle arrived, Jussi and I hurried into it, but unfortunately, Maria could not follow us quickly enough, so that the boat left the shore and Maria was left behind. We waited on our side for Maria coming with the next boat, but she did not come. To find her, we went back and searched for her many hours, but in vain. Ultimately, full of anxiety, we headed for our hotel to inform the children about what had happened. To our extreme happiness, we saw Maria there in a very good mood in talk with Tara and Ina. She told us that she had immediately left the place and walked back to the hotel. Fortunately, she met some nuns going in the same direction of the Lower Circular Road. Later we came to know that Mother Teresa lived in the same locality of our hotel. It was a happy end for us. To celebrate the occasion, I looked for my bottle of Johnnie Walker, which I had bought on our flight. To my surprise, my whisky was not in the place where I had kept it. I asked Tara and Ina if they had hidden or taken it. Suddenly, I saw our service boy lying unconsciously drunk on the floor of the hotel. The boy was a near relative of the owner of this hotel, who expressed his apology for his bad conduct. He offered me even compensation for the said whisky. We all felt very sorry for that boy. We imagined the frustrations of the millions of young men in this city who become addicted to the dangerous local alcohol and drugs to forget the failures and sorrows of life. At the time of our departure for Shakra, we saw thousands of refugees from Bangladesh staying and loitering hungrily at Howrah Station.

We reached my village in 1974 on a train with a coal engine, and now the trains were largely electrified and were running much faster for longer distances and provided even air-conditioned compartments with food service. The hawkers (wallas) were not allowed to offer their products anymore in such trains. But the ticket prices were very high, and seat reservations in advance became compulsory. On short distances, common people traveled on a passenger train or bus. Our village had also changed a lot. The younger ones had migrated to the Indian cities and abroad. The village was inhabited largely by older people, women, and children. But the inhabitants looked better fed, clad, and lived mostly in solid houses. Some of the younger members of our family were already there to welcome us and keep us company. Ina took some pictures of our family members, the house, and the landscape. Those pictures were later published under the title "Das Dorf meines Vaters" (My father's village) in the ADAC Reise-Magazine, Nr. 90, 2006, then one of the biggest travel journals of Germany.

From Shakra we went to Damla, where my second sister Tara lived with her family. Maria and the children had never been there. Whenever I came to Shakra alone or with my family, she had always come for a visit from Damla to Shakra, some 120 km. Her village is near the border of Nepal on the bank of the river Bhagmati, which we had seen before in Kathmandu in 1974. It is a monsoon and flood area, as many rivers come down there from Nepal and Tibet. Our children wanted to see my sister's home and this very much undeveloped part of India. The Champaran district is near to Damla. As a result of the American Civil War (1776) and the French Revolution (1789) leading to the uprisings of the slaves of the carribic islands, the East India Company brought hundreds of British, French and Dutch planters to the slump area of the Ganges to cultivate indigo for the British cotton industries and for the navy who wore blue uniforms. Mahatma Gandhi began his first non-violence movement (Satyagraha) in 1917 in Champaran against the exploitation of the planters.

Traveling to Damla by jeep took us nearly a full day on the muddy roads and newly bad constructed dams. We had to stop several times because the jeep had to be repaired. Inspite of all these troubles, we enjoyed the view of the fields, the farmers, the harvest, the dams, and the rivers. Tara's family members had prepared well for our stay. The rooms were white-washed, the anti-septic toilette was ready and the generator was working. A fisherman (mallah) came with his net to take some Himalayan fish out of their pond, which was grilled before our eyes. In front of my sister's house, we noticed marihuana (bhang) growing wild in abundance. The seeds had come there by the wind and the excrements of the birds from Nepal. Just for fun, the children wanted to take some of the marihuana back to Germany, but realized soon the legal risk of transportation. For the first time, they saw the aboriginals (adivasis), who usually came from Orissa (1,000 km away) to work on the field of landowners of this Tirhut area. The adivasis were small, thin, and half-naked. They even ate rats, dead animals and slept on the bare fields. This part of India (Tirhut) is very fertile. The biggest zamindar of India, the Maharaja of Darbhanga lived there and had the British administrator Gerald Danby for his land. This area is also reputed for its better-educated class of Maithil Brahmins who spoke Sanskrit and English and worked as priests and Pundits in the temples of India, while the modern educated ones went mostly to the United States of America. After some time, we left Damla to visit my second sister in Patna,130 km. Now our jeep was full of bags with grain for my sister in Patna, who owned some land in Damla. On our way to Patna, Jussi got high fever with chills. Was that malaria? We did not know exactly where he could have got it, in Bihar or Kolkata? That time it took us less time to cross the Ganges as a bridge called Gandhi Bridge had been completed in 1982. It is 5,730 m long, the longest of its kind in Asia. We lived with my sister Gurya in an apartment of the Patliputra colony, some 8 km from the main city of Patna. It was primarily built for British residents and administrative purposes, is situated on the bank of the Ganges. The British made the residences, offices, clubs, convents for boys and girls, churches, and dispensaries. In this area, it is still possible to get modern education of all kinds. But I also heard of a lot of disputes about property in this Patliputra colony, as the residences and lands of the people, who had migrated to western countries have been occupied illegally by others with the co-operation of the local authorities. I saw a very fine newly built house adjacent to the apartment of my sister. She told me that the house had been built with stolen material of the Gandhi Bridge and the owner of the house was an engineer working there. At the same time, she complained that she was married to a teacher and not to an engineer, otherwise, she would also have a house like that. We visited practically all the places worth-seeing in Patna, such as Gandhi Maidan, Gole Ghar (round store room), the Secretariat, and the Patna Museum, which is unique for the remains and sculptures of Greco-Buddhist influences from the Gandhara Period (1st to 5th century B.C.). The children explored their own Patna market, the Tara Planetarium, and the Holy Kurji Hospital, which is also open to people with little means. I remember that Jussi went to the Patna Zoo with his cousin Sunny, where he was shown a white tiger, cobra, neem (tree with branches used as a toothbrush), and an old peepal tree (revered as God), growing hardly anywhere else than in India. For the first time in his life, Jussi rode an elephant there. Maria and I visited the headmaster of Saint Michael School, an American missionary high school, to give him some money for a poor child in that school on behalf of his sister in Germany. Later we came to know that this missionary school was exclusively attended by boys whose parents paid an exorbitant amount of yearly fee and donations for admission in this school.

The Bodh Gaya is only 96 km from Patna, therefore we decided not to miss this historical place where Gautama Buddha (566 – 486 B. C.) lived and meditated under the Bodhi (enlightenment) tree. We visited in the way to Bodh Gaya, the Buddhist University of Nalanda, which was attended and mentioned by the famous Chinese Buddhist monks Fa-Hien (401 – 410) and Hiuen-Tsang (630 – 643). We hired a taxi and went first to Pawapuri, where Mahavira founded the Jaina religion in the sixth century B.C. The followers of this religion count only six to seven million, are known for its strict adherence to non-violence (ahimsa) way of life, but they are the richest tradesmen in India. In Pawapuri, we saw the monasteries, temples and a pond full of holy fish, never intended to be fished. And then we drove to Bodh Gaya and opened our boxes of food to eat. It was so hot there that our boiled eggs and the bananas, given to us a few hours ago in Patna became uneatable. We saw the Mahabodhi temple, the Lotus pond from the time of Buddha, and plenty of poor devotees, coming on foot from Sri Lanka, Nepal, and Tibet, cooked their food, slept on the road and under the Bodhi tree, where Buddha had once meditated. On our return to Patna, we took a break in the city of Gaya to buy some water and fruit. Suddenly we had to hurry back to our car on the request of our driver to leave the place immediately. After some minutes, our driver stopped the car at a lonely place, and we saw him talking with another driver. He told us that while he had parked the car at the market, he had slightly touched his car in the rear. Both drivers had run away from the place of the accident because they were afraid of being questioned by the local police. The police would have stopped them unnecessarily and would have extorted from them an exorbitant amount of bribery by threatening them to keep them in a jail. Therefore, they had both run away quickly from the place of the incident and could now settle the matter amicably amongst them. I knew about this common way of settling disputes among the people of India. After our return to Patna, we prepared ourselves for our journey to Mumbai. Tara and Ina wanted to leave Patna earlier to visit some place on their way to Mumbai. I advised them to stop at Allahabad, now Paryag,160 km from Patna. This city was founded in 1553 by Akbar the Great. The place is famous for its Kumbh Mela (Nectar Feast), held at Triveni, where the three rivers Ganges, Jamuna, and the invisible Saraswati meet. Here Jawaharlal Nehru (1889-1964) was born and lived in his ancestral house of Anand Bhavan (happy house). Tara and Ina went there for a night to Allahabad and we met them a day later in Mumbai as agreed. Maria, Jussi, and I waited for them them in the Leopold Café in Colaba, a refreshment and food shop, highly visited by European tourists. Just adjacent to it, we stayed in the hotel Godwin. By that time, the hotels in Mumbai had become modern and were categorized in star hotels. The British got Mumbai from Portugal as a wedding gift in 1661.This place being nearer to Africa and Europe, developed as the greatest commercial port city of India. The old traders of Parsis, Banias, Jainas, Bohras, Khojas, and Memons of Gujarat came and settled in the city to trade with overseas countries of the whole world. From here, they were brought by the British or sailed themselves to Africa for work and trade. Thus, the place became a highly cosmopolitan and industrial city.The British established first the joint-stock companies in Mumbai with the financial help of these trading communities. Mumbai emerged as the main city of shipping, banks, insurances, textiles, alcohol, tobacco, and opium, which were by large first traded by Parsis from Mumbai. Our children visited the Victoria Terminal Station, built-in 1888 in an Indo-Saracen style, the Gate of India, constructed in 1911 to welcome King Georg V and Queen Mary. They traveled by a ferry from the India Gate to see the Elephanta Cave, known for its massive and high (7m) Shiva Statue. Tara and Ina seized the opportunity to travel from Mumbai to Goa to see its beaches, hippies, and the remains of its Portuguese heritage. After they had come back from Goa, we were invited together by my friend Prakash and his wife Shantu and her daughter Anjeli to a gorgeous restaurant at Malabar Hill. Before our departure from Mumbai, we went to visit the Tower of Silence (Dhakma) in the Malabar Hills, where the Parsis threw corpses for the vultures to feed on. The place was closed and looked deserted. We came to know that, due to the massive use of fertilizers in agriculture, the vultures had been decimated for this purpose, and the community of Parsi was now thinking of the alternative way of cremation. With old and new memories of the city, we left Mumbai with a feeling of uncertainty, if we would ever come together to India again.

1996 Tara visited India with her friend Roland. At that time, I was in Patna and she came to meet me there for a few days. From her earlier visits, she knew my relatives and the city well. I went with her to Kumhara, the ancient city of Patliputra of the Mauryan age, 12 km away. An entry gate was there, but nobody was present to show us or inform us about the ancient capital. Suddenly a watchman appeared, who was more interested in selling some fake coins and remnants of the Mauryan period than in showing us something historical. Sometime ago, I met accidently a German archeologist there, who told me that his findings, even the old bricks and wooden rotten pieces of the palaces, were stolen at night. Tara went alone to visit the city of Patna and purchased some clothes and handicrafts in the market. Gurya told me once, that the tradesmen of the market remembered Tara as a European girl who came to choose and buy things alone. I remember that Gurya waited impatiently for her in the evening hours and sent her servants to look after her in the nearby streets of Patliputra colony. My sister told me once that Tara dropped secretly many Charrinis, a fourth of the silver coin of a rupee, into her saving mug.

1997 Ina visited me, also alone in India. She came directly from Delhi to Patna to see me and stayed with me for some days and to visit my village Shakra too. After a short stay with her in Patna, we went to Shakra. My mother was still alive. For the first time, we took a bus from Patna, which went directly to our village. As a precautionary measure, I bought all three tickets on one side of the bus, so that we had more place to sit. The bus became soon crowded with people standing and sitting on the roof with luggage. The passengers in the bus occupied our seats without asking us, and a woman put her two kids at Ina's lap. Ina saw such a rush in a bus for the first time, the passengers pushing and pressing to find a place in the bus. It took more than six hours to cover the distance of about 120 km from Patna to Shakra. In spite of the tiresome journey, Ina was joyous to see my mother, my sister Tara, the house and the surroundings once again.

She saw very little changes there since her last visit in 1993. I slept on the veranda and Ina near to me in a room. Without asking Ina, Tara slept in the same room with Ina. It is unusual for a woman in India to sleep without a company of the same sex, or to let somebody sleep alone.

After a stay of two nights, we left Shakra with my mother for Patna. We avoided a bus this time and took a passenger train to Patna. Such local trains are full of daily commuters, students, and sellers of grains, vegetables and small animals for the markets of the nearby towns and cities. On such local trains, the people travel mostly without tickets, sit in the aisles, on top of the roof of the train, hang on the doors and pull the breaks to get off at the places of their choices. The ticket inspectors are mainly interested in collecting bribes and vegetables from the sellers. It was very interesting for Ina to see such scenes. We left our train in Hajipur and hired a rickshaw for the Patliputra colony in Patna,15 km from Hajipur. We crossed the Ganges Bridge, which Ina had already seen before. Somewhere our rickshaw was stopped by a traffic officer under the pretence of fast driving. We were kept detained in front of a tea shop, where the officer sat patiently, eating and drinking his tea. The driver was threatened with abuses and threatened the confiscation of his rickshaw. The poor driver became so afraid that he begged us for extra money to bribe the officer. After a delay of more than an hour and the payment of a whole day's earning of the driver, we were allowed to continue our travel. Ina had never seen such an act of robbery by a police officer in daylight and the ruthless suppression of the working class in India. During our sojourn in Patliputra, my sister Gurya suddenly suffered from pain and was brought to the Holy Kurji Hospital, where, according to the diagnosis of a doctor, a stone in her gall bladder had to be removed at once. She had to pay in advance for the stay in the hospital and the operation cost, otherwise, the admission to the hospital had not been permitted. After her release from the hospital, she showed me the stone that had been taken out from her. Most of the Indians do not believe in such operations, as they believe that the doctors invent such operations and show fake stones to the patients. This time Ina met my cousins Tara, Boby, and other close relatives. She sadly watched the poor patients outside of the Holy Kurji Hospital waiting day and night together with their sick relatives for admission in the hospital. My sister Gurya had since long had a female servant, who was deaf and dumb (Batahia), she was nameless and nobody knew from where she came. Ina was always kind to her, caressing her cheek and hair. Whenever I meet the Batahia alone, she asked me about Ina's welfare and whereabouts, in gestures.

2002 Jussi ended his studies of medicine in Hamburg and chose for his practical training in the renowned "All India Institute of Medical Sciences" (AIIMS) in Delhi. He traveled there with another medical trainee from Hamburg named Thorsten. When I met them a little bit later in Delhi, they felt well accommodated in a small hotel of Delhi and learned some words of Hindustani for daily purposes. They admired the doctors of the AIIMS, who were qualified ideologists and took good care of the poor patients of India. Jussi and Thorsten were surprised to see monkeys moving around freely on the compound of this hospital and in the doctors' rooms. After the end of their training, they decided to visit my sister in Patna. We hired a car from our hotel to the New Delhi Railway Station and soon noticed that the driver did not know the direction of the station. When we asked him about his ignorance and he told us that he had come from his state of Haryana to Delhi only yesterday. As he knew driving, the car owner employed him and had sent him to drive us to the station. Perplexed and angry with this situation, we hired a rickshaw man, who drove in front of our taxi to guide him to the station. Thus, with our car behind the rickshaw driver, we reached the New Delhi station, just a few minutes before our train started for Patna. During our stay in Patna, Gurya extended her hospitability to Thorsten equally. She provided the same type of bed, pillows, and mosquito net for both the boys. She told me that Thorsten was a friend of your son and your son is my nephew; therefore, it was my duty to treat Thorsten in the same way as Jussi. After a stay in Patna, I accompanied Jussi and Thorsten to Darjeeling, as they wished to see a British hill station of India. After reaching the last station of Siliguri, they did not like to travel for eight hours on the Toy Train and preferred to travel by taxi to Darjeeling. Jussi remembered little from his earlier trip as a child to Darjeeling in 1978, but now he enjoyed the sight of the valley, the tea gardens, and the little agricultural fields on the slopes of the mountain. In Darjeeling, we stayed in a state tourist house with bed tea, and breakfast. Jussi and Thorsten went to see the places of British times and bought clothes and shoes from street sellers, which came from China and were cheaper. They wanted to have a glimpse at Mount Everest, the highest peak of the world (8884m). To see it, they took a jeep with some other Europeans for Tiger Hill, 32 km from the center. They stayed at Tiger Hill for a night and were taken before sunrise to have a clear glance at Mount Everest. After seeing most of Darjeeling, we took a taxi back to Siliguri for our return by train to Patna. That time we traveled in a common third-class bogey, as the boys wished to make the experience of traveling with the masses. We sat on our wooden benches sandwiched between people of all kinds, who were mostly on the way to nearby working towns. In the middle of the night, Thorsten wished to go to the toilet, and I showed him the way to go there. But he came back quickly and told me that two or three persons were sleeping inside the toilet. I went to the place with him and asked the sleeping men to vacate the toilet room for some time. After coming back from the toilet, Thorsten asked me how several people could sleep so patiently in a small toilet room of a train, whereas millions of Europeans could not sleep in good beds without taking sleeping pills. I told him that the poor in India had very little place to sleep in their houses in a village, and in the cities they slept together with many others, even in shifts in a very small room (kholi). I accompanied Jussi and Thorsten from Patna to Delhi. As they had very little time to see Delhi, I took the opportunity to show them some famous parts of Delhi such as Qutub Minar, a 73 m high tower, built by the first Turkish sultan in 1192 and the Bahai Temple. I went with Jussi to the emporiums in Janpath, Connaught Place, where he bought tea, engraved wooden boxes, brass materials, and chess pieces in ivory. After three months of training, Jussi and Thorsten left Delhi with a lot of medical experiences and memories of the land and the people of India.

2006 Jussi had become a doctor of medicine and came for a holiday to the hill station of Kalimpong, 52 km from Darjeeling. Kalimpong used to be an entry door to Tibet and a quarter of the British army. Maria and I had flown to Kalimpong some days earlier than Jussi. Now Maria was a retired teacher. We stayed in Kalimpong in a boarding house named Dixie, where mostly young boys and girls from America lived. Jussi did not like to stay at Dixie, as it did not provide him with much of the calm and rest, which he needed after his strenuous job in the hospital and a long exhausting flight with stopovers from Hamburg to Kalimpong. Therefore we agreed to stay with him in the Himalayan Hotel, which had once been the residence of a British tradesman. Edmund Hillary (1919-2008), the first climber of Mount Everest had stayed there with his team. As I liked to visit my family members in Bihar, I left Maria and Jussi in Kalimpong, where they stayed for a couple of days, and from there, they went to Darjeeling. They stayed in the hotel Windamere of Darjeeling for a couple of days, where Jussi used the solitude and quietness of that hotel on the top of a mountain to prepare for his other medical examinations. Maria and Jussi still remember the old British-style chimney and the warm pillows given to them every night in the hotel. I came first from Bihar to Delhi, and later they arrived from Darjeeling. In Delhi, we stayed together in the hotel Broadway of Old Delhi, near Darya Ganj. Jussi rested there too, whereas Maria and I visited the old churches as the Holy Trinity Church, the St. James Church and went to nearby Jama Masjid (Friday mosque), built by Shah Jahan. This is the biggest Indian mosque, with a hall to pray for 25,000 people. We visited my nieces and nephews, who were either studying or working in Delhi. We also met our friends from earlier days, such as Guptas, Sharma, Fahim, and Khan, who had visited us in between in Bremen.

Here I must tell you of a happening in Delhi that we still remember. For a long time, we had known a very rich family of traders there. During our stay in the hotel Broadway, the family members of the traders told me of a tragedy. A girl of the family came to know a boy through chats on the internet and fell in love with him, but the boy did not belong to her caste, and the girl went away with the boy to an unknown place. Such things as love and marriage out of the caste happen, but are seldom allowed by the parents in India. They are droven away from the family, even tortured and murdered. They approached me to ask a friend of mine for urgent assistance, who at that time was serving as a Chief Secretary of the President of India. The secretary was not only a very high civil servant but belonged as well to a very old aristocratic ruling family of India. This person should insist the Chief Police Officer of Delhi to do more to find out the whereabouts of this missing girl. The girl's father was willing to pay any sum to the police to get his daughter back to marry her to a man of her caste. In the course of the talks, we came to know that the girl was not minor anymore. According to Indian law, she was free to decide independently. When we left the house of this aristocrat, at least 15 people were waiting for him in submissive postures in front of his house. At that moment, Jussi was there with me and was very much surprised to see such humble petitioners. The humility and subjucation of the lower by the upper castes had been practiced for centuries. It can be traced in the earliest Sanskrit writing of Arthasastras (principles of earthly rule) of Kautilya from the fourth century B. C. and of a French physician Francois Bernier at the courts of the Moghuls in "Travels in the Mughal Empire" (1656–1668). Thank God, the missing girl was found. A groom was quickly arranged for her in the same caste of her family. We were invited to attend the marriage ceremony in Delhi. We went to Delhi and stayed in their house. Maria was bestowed with the privilege to be invited at the special wedding ceremony, which was exclusively attended by the nearest women of the family. We did not know how much money had been offered in advance to the bridegroom, but we saw Mercedes and Mitsubishi cars as presents (dowry) to her. We were taken with a Mercedes to their family farm, 20 km in south from Delhi. There the wedding was celebrated with great pomp and grandeur with hundreds of guests. According to a horoscope (patra) of a Pundit, the wedding took place in the month of December in the mentioned farm, where it was very cold and windy.

Maria caught a very severe coldness, so we left Delhi quickly for her treatment in Germany, but we still enjoy to re-collect this episode with a happy end for the family.

2007 Ina came to India on behalf of a travel agency, to find out about some holiday resorts near Mumbai for a German journal. She came from Mumbai to meet me in Delhi for a day only. In spite of the short time, we went to see the Gandhi Memorial (samadhi) at Raj Ghat at Yamuna River, where Ina had never been before. I showed her as well the Lodhi Garden, tombs of Lodhi kings(1451-1526), the rulers before the Mughals in India and went to the nearby posh Khan Market, where she bought clothes and gifts for her children. We ate together in an Italian restaurant there. Finally, she was taken back to the Domestic Airport of Delhi by Gopal, the driver of Guptas, whom Ina knew.

2008 Tara arrived in India shortly after Ina. Maria, and I were also in Delhi , so we went to the airport of Delhi together to pick her up. We took her to our hotel, the “India International Centre (IIC)”, built by the Government of India for national and international journalists. The IIC is situated in very beautiful surroundings of Delhi, such as the Habitat Center, Lodhi Garden, Khan Market, and the Goethe House, which was earlier called Friedrich Max Müller Bhavan after the German-born philologist and orientalist (1823-1900). We could stay there as our friend Sharma was a member of this society. Maria and Tara visited Khan Market und Lodhi Market for the first time. We went together to the Goethe Institute, where we saw many Indian students in its courtyard and German library and took our meal in the cafeteria of this Institute.

As Tara had never been before to Chandigarh, the capital city of the two states Haryana and Punjab, we booked our tickets on the Shatabdi Express for Chandigarh. The Shatabdi Express is now one of the best fast trains in India, with air-conditioned compartments, and its passengers are served with bottled mineral waters, newspapers, breakfast, and food with ice cream. The city of Chandigarh is 260 km away from Delhi, and it takes less than five hours to travel there. The city was founded in a mountainous area of Shivalik by the French architect Le Corbusier, a friend of Jawaharlal Nehru. It is the first city of India to have been planned in sectors, residential areas, gardens, administrative areas, and shopping centers. We stayed there in the Hotel Shivalik with breakfast and dinner. The possibility to have breakfast and evening meals had only recently started in some hotels of India. We saw the Assembly House, Secretariat, and Court, planned by Corbusier in his lifetime and visited the museum with sketches of architectural plans of him. We walked for hours in the bougainvillea, rose, and plantation gardens with plentiful varieties of plantations and herbs, hardly to be seen elsewhere in India. We went to visit the unique Rock Garden with its clay and stone sculptures, mostly made by the local artist Neck Chand. Then we walked along the recreational Sukhna Lake, stretching in the midst of the Shivalik mountains. We hired a boat and a boatman, who showed us the surroundings of the lake. In Chandigarh, I met a person whom I knew from my time in Köln through my friend Bali, now living in Wuppertal. He had retired from his position of chancellor of the University of Chandigarh. He invited us to his golf club, where we had an afternoon lunch and talked about the university of Köln (Cologne) and our mutual friends there. He invited us for a meal with his family members at his residence. Maria talked with his wife and Tara with her daughter, and came to know through them a lot about this new city, its surroundings and developments. We saw accidently from his house the toy train going to Shimla, some 96 km, the resort of British administrators and governors. In the busiest shopping sector 17 of Chandigarh, we bought our presents for Germany and Tara visited very likely the coffee house, general stores and book shops, which were full of modern books of Indian writers. We still remember that Maria had once had her shoes polished in that sector by a boy to help him earn some money. After the polishing, the boy insisted on asking for much more money than fixed with him. The boy said to Maria that she had not understood the price properly and that the sum he had told her before had been for only one of her shoes. A lot of polishing boys gathered around us to make us pay what the boy demanded. At the tourist office in sector 17, we were told that the boys were employed and trained by gangsters to blackmail and harass the foreign tourists, and the local police worked with them. We never expected that in this modern city, the gangsters had free rein to abuse the tourists and poor children of India. After seeing most of its interesting places and stay in the Shivalik Hotel, we left Chandigarh via Delhi to return to Germany.

2011 we accompanied Ina and her two daughters Lilia and Matilda, age nine and seven, to India. We had seen India with our daughter Ina several times before. Now she wanted to take her children to India to show them the birthplace, the relatives, and the country of her grandfather. The children Lilia and Matilda wanted us to come along with them. Ina flew with her children from Hamburg, and Maria and I from Bremen to meet them in Amsterdam for our further travel together to Delhi. With KLM, we reached Delhi at 01.00 a.m., in the very late hours of the night. We waited at Delhi airport till morning, as our train to Mussoorie via Dehradun left at 06.00 a. m. New Delhi railway station. We had already booked our tickets on the internet in Bremen, which was possible now. Considering the comfort of the children, we had booked on the Shatabdi Express. Having been awake the nights before in air and airport, the children slept deeply in the compartment and missed the drinks and the good breakfast served in this train. To reach Mussoorie, we had to travel first to Dehradun, 283 km from Delhi. Dehradun is a city where the British had military posts to guard borders with China and Tibet, and built cantonments, convents, and schools for their civil servants. These institutions are still used by the ruling elite of India. In Dehradun we hired two taxis for our drive of 38 km to Mussoorie, 2,200 m high. The children were in that hilly region for the first time and became very excited to see the Himalayan ranges, curves, houses, fields, flowers, and monkeys on the trees of the mountains. In the city of Mussoorie, we were picked up by the staff of the hotel Kasamanda, which had earlier belonged to a Maharaja of a nearby state. To get to the hotel on the top of a mountain, a car of the hotel was always available, but the children seldom used it and enjoyed a walk there. Ina went with her children to show them the mall, convents, churches, bungalows, towers, and the wild natural reserves. In the evening, we walked together to Gandhi Chowk for our meal with pakoras, samosas, puris, and vegetables from there. Maria took Ina and her children for a walk to the Camel Back Road, a tour of 6 km, showed them the oldest British cemetery, the newly built ashrams, temples, and the hotel, where Maria and I had stayed years before. The Camel Road is visited only by those who prefer loneliness, solitude, and walking a longer distance. At the end of the road, there were ponies, donkeys and horses for a ride along the Camel Back Road. From Mussoorie, we went by taxi to Rishikesh,

80 km. We stayed in the hotel "Ganga ke kinare" (on the side of the Ganges). Undoubtedly, the hotel was right in front of the Ganges and we could see the river, the pilgrims, prayers, boats, lamps, and feasts in honor of the holy river from our windows. But our hotel was nearly empty, as Indians hardly stay in hotels and the Europeans prefer ashrams and yoga centers as resorts. Rishikesh is the place where the Ganges comes down from the ravines of the Himalayas; therefore, it is revered as a sacred place from the devotees of the river. You see there are some Europeans in the costumes of sadhus, sanyas, yogis, and beggars. Lilia and Matilda had their first experience to see such a rush of pilgrims, religious utensils, talisman, holy cows, and monkeys moving together freely without fear of each other. The children enjoyed the crossing of the Ram Jhula Pul (rope bridge) over the Ganges along with the pilgrims and holy animals. Maria and I met an Indian lawyer who came here every year from London to live in an ashram, and he introduced us to his guru. Ina and her children saw the market and meditation center on the bank of the Ganges. We saw them accidently in the midst of the busy market and went for a meal with them in the most famous vegetarian restaurant, known as Chotiwala. In the evening, we also went to eat together in a very small vegetarian restaurant, which had been recently started by a young girl and was mostly frequented by European girls. One evening, we saw a procession of a wedding ceremony from our hotel. The musicians with drums, sarangi and trumpets and lamps on their heads were moving slowly along the Ganges with the bridegroom, sitting on a white horse with marigolds and ornaments. By seeing this Ina and her children became so much excited that they ran behind the procession and followed the wedding group for some time. It is very common in India that festivals of joy and sorrow are celebrated on the banks of the Ganges. Perhaps

it reminds the Indians of their hereditary affiliation to the holy river, as the poet Mohammad Iqbal (1877-1938) wrote in Urdu: "Oh water of the Ganga, do you remember that we all coming from somewhere to India, sheltered first under your branches". After seeing Rishikesh, we took a taxi to Haridwar early in the morning. From Rishikesh to Haridwar, there is a distance of only 80 km, but to reach Bihar, we had to travel first from Rishikesh via Haridwar to Delhi, 235 km away. We had no time to visit Haridwar, where die Ganges meets the real flat land of India. Thus, Haridwar is, after Varanasi, the second holiest place for the Hindus, where the Kumbh Mela takes place every twelve years there. At the railway station of New Delhi, our friends were waiting to put us on the train to Shakra, some 870 km. We had already booked a compartment for us because of the long travel time of 18 hours. As soon as we reached Shakra, the children were surrounded by the village people, especially by the smaller ones, as they had never seen before white girls. Lilia and Matilda were much delighted to see the house of my childhood and the village of my birth, and its rural surroundings. Having little time, we stayed in Shakra for a night. The children received some ornaments from my nearest kin with the request to keep them as a heritage of the family. We left the place for Patna, as our grandchildren wanted to visit their aunt Gurya. We stayed in the hotel Windsor of Patna. Ina knew the city well enough to show her children and went with them to the Tara Planetarium, the Patna Market, Gol Ghar, Gandhi Maidan, Patna museum, etc. Together we visited Patna Zoo and took its small train for a round trip. To see the tiger, beer, snake charmer, and the marriage ceremony of the monkeys. We visited Gurya and her husband, her very old servant batahia was already dead. Gurya was not feeling well enough to go shopping, so she gave some money to Lilia and Matilda to buy clothes and get them ready in Delhi. On our departure from Patna, Gurya and her husband accompanied us to the station of Patna. That was the last time that Maria and Ina saw them.

Our next program from Patna was to Agra, for which we had in advance also booked tickets with sleeping beds in compartments with air condition. After having traveled so often by train, Ina wanted to take a flight from Patna to Agra, which I could understand well, because the train would take 18 hours for 800 km. Unfortunately, there was no direct flight from Patna to Agra but a stop of one night in Delhi and a stay in a hotel at the airport, a flight for Agra was possible from Patna. And it took more than 24 hours altogether, with a total cost of more than a hundred dollars per person, whereas we paid just 16 dollars for a train ticket per person in an air-conditioned sleeping compartment from Patna to Agra. All these factors considered, it appeared useless to travel by air, so Ina decided to travel by train with us together. The train passed Varanasi on the way to Agra. From the train, we could see the main coast of the Ganges and had a good glimpse of pilgrims and happenings on the Ganges. We all slept well on our seats throughout the night. I saw Lilia in the early morning looking out of the window and counting the numbers of the persons who were defecating near the rails. One could observe this kind of activity throughout India, especially in the morning hours from a train. In Agra, we stayed in the Hotel Amar. This town, which is near to the desert of Rajasthan, remains hot and humid most of the year. The children used the swimming pool of the hotel frequently. Ina went with them to Taj Mahal, Red Fort, and peacock gardens and we went to see the Havelis in old Agra. Ina invited us to a restaurant named Shanti, about which she had read in the Lonely Planet. On our way to the Shanti, Matilda fell into a ditch at the entrance of this restaurant. We managed to get some water there, and after cleaning her up, we entered the restaurant. The place was full of young European tourists. We asked for an Italian dish, which was served after a long time, and it was cold and not tasty. Noticing our dissatisfaction of the food, the owner wanted to give us back the money, which, we of course, refused to accept. Maria promised to send him an original Italian recipe. Lilia and Matilda bought a small Taj Mahal for me from a street vendor, and presented this with so much affection, that I still remember the joyous moment. With the children's school holidays approaching the end, we left Agra for Delhi via the holy city of Mathura on the river Jamuna. In Delhi, we got off at the station of Nizamuddin Aulia, where the greatest sufi of India had lived and preached in the 14th century and was buried. In Delhi, we had booked the Hotel Parkland in the Defence Colony of South Delhi, a calm and quiet residential area of the Indian military. From there, Sharma drove us to a new uninhabited area with forests of East Noida, where he intended to buy his new apartment. He showed us the huge building in construction and invited us to a restaurant in his golf club. Still today, the children remember this restaurant with its rotating tables and large number of Indian dishes. Pranav, the grandson of our oldest friend Gupta in Delhi, invited us to a newly opened restaurant, the Parikrama, on the top of a building in Connaught Place, which rotated around Delhi. Lilia and Matilda were amazed to discover Delhi from all four sides. In the evening, we finally went with the children to Chandni Chowk, the busiest market in Asia, where most of the gold and silver ornaments of the world are sold.

The Chandni Chowk (Moonlight Square) is situated on old Delhi, opposite of the Red Fort (Lal Qila), built by Shah Jahan (1639-1648) and the Jamuna River, coming from the Himalayas and meeting the Ganges after 1,376 km in Allahabad. It is widely said that Its water remained largely unpolluted till the end of the Moghul Empire in 1857. The people living along the Jamuna kept its water clean, as the same water was used as drinking water by the kings and emperors in Delhi.

While we were walking around Chandni Chowk, Lilia and Matilda saw a dog following us for minutes, and the children could not understand why an unknown dog would follow us and were scared of its presence. After some time, the dog left us and disappeared. In my opinion, the dog had perhaps lived for some time with a European family in Chandni Chowk, who went back to his home and left the dog with somebody there. Perhaps this dog was looking for its old masters, and at the sight of white faces, the dog had thought by mistake to have found again his former owners. As the return flight to Germany was at 3.00 a.m. at night, so Pranav took us to his family in Greater Kailash, where we passed the waiting time with him and his family members, and our children played with the offsprings of Guptas. We were taken to the airfield by both Sharma and Pranav. Maria, Lilia, and Matilda took the plane to Amsterdam, and I remained in Delhi for a few days more to stay with Sharma in Noida, as we had been planning that for a long time.

2013 Tara wanted to show India to her daughter Dina too. She was then 15 years old, and Tara wanted us as well to accompany them. Therefore, Tara, Dina, Maria, and I flew together to India and landed in Delhi at 3.00 a.m. It is usual that the planes from Europe arrive in and depart from Delhi mostly late at night. Gopal took us directly from the airport to the new railway station of Anand Bihar. From there the train left at 6.00 in the early morning for Nainital via Kathgodam, a railway station in the valley of Himalaya, 330 km away from Delhi. Neither Maria nor Tara had ever been there before. We waited for a few hours in the waiting room of Anand Bihar, till our train came for Kathgodam. A lot of passengers relaxed there congested, talked to each other, slept, and snored. Maria and Tara felt uneasy there, but Dina kept herself busy with her mobile and remained undisturbed by the many disturbances and noises of the waiting room. Our train was on time and we arrived in Kathgodam in five hours, hired a taxi for Nainital (25 km) and reached our hotel in one hour. The Hotel Naini Retreat was situated on the top of a hill at the height of 2,000 m with a direct view on the Lake Naini. The hotel provided breakfast and dinner so that we did not need to look for a restaurant somewhere in the night. We could recover there from the long journey. Most hotels at hill stations offer their guests transport possibility to the mall of the place.Therefore, we could visit the city and the surroundings of the lake. Nainital (valley of the eyes), being near to the state of Uttar Pradesh (U. P.), shows more Indian influences than British, as the British had preferred Darjeeling, Mussoorie, and Shimla as holiday resorts. Once, we used the ropeway, which takes you higher in the mountain in seven or eight minutes. We went together with this ropeway and saw a small zoo with birds, a café and the Nainital below from there. Going back down, Dina and I used the same ropeway, but Maria and Tara decided to walk down to see the slope in detail. Dina and I waited for Maria and Tara for an hour, in vain. Ultimately, when they arrived, they told us that on the way down a lot of people and animals lived on the slopes in small huts and tents and even farmed on the hills. Therefore, it had not been easy to find a way down. This reminded me of a personal experience in India. I once lived in Agra behind the Agra Fort and wanted to go from there to the Taj Mahal. I asked an old banana seller for the way to the Taj. The vendor told me that he had been driven out of the area of the Taj a long time ago and he was not allowed by the police to sell things like bananas there. For him, there is now two Agra: one for the tourists and the other one for a poor man like him. Thus, we saw an expensive ropeway for the tourists in Nainital, from where the masses of people living below it could not be seen. On our own, we visited some of the sights near Nainital, as Garhi Mandir (temple) and a big Hanuman statue, a God with the head of an elephant. On our departure from Nainital we hired a taxi for Moradabad for our journey by train to Lucknow.On the way to Moradabad, we stopped at Rampur to visit the Reza Library, known for its rare Muslim manuscripts and miniature paintings collected by the Nawabs of this former state. Unfortunately, the library was being renovated. The head of this library, a lady of the family of a Nawab, appeared to express her apologies for that. Because of an European teenager dress and outfit. Dina became the attraction of the schoolgirls there who were covered in their burqas and hijabs. We left Rampur and reached Moradabad to catch our train to Lucknow, 346 km. Inspite of the distance, the journey with the Shatabdi Express to Lucknow was comfortable. We passed through the city of Kanpur on the Ganges, known for its leather products. We reached Lucknow in the late evening and went directly to our hotel Clark Awadh. Lucknow was ruled in the 18th and 19th centuries by the Nawabs, who were Schias, and had originally come from Iran. In the Mutiny of 1857, they were overthrown by the British. A lot of monumental and worship places of the Shias are to be seen here, such as Bara Imambara (house of Great Imams), the Rumi Darwaza (doors like in Rom), and tombs and music schools. The last Nawab Wajid Ali Shah of Lucknow was a creator of Kathak dance and Thumri songs, which is the most famous one in north India. The most important from colonial era is the Residency, where the British lived in Lucknow with soldiers. In this place, the mutiny of Indian sepoys (soldiers) was fought in 1857, killing more than 2,000 British soldiers. We saw the damages and bullet holes in walls of the British Residency. We remember that, in the courtyard of the Residency, Dina was followed and stared at by some curious boys. We did not like such behavior and tried to chase the boys away from her. But Dina did not care about of the boys according to the motto "to see and to be seen". We went some 15 km away from our hotel to a convent, built by the French on the bank of the river Gomti in 1845, called La Martinière taught and lived as an adviser to the Nawabs against the British. The architecture is a masterpiece of Indo- European construction and a witness to the era of hegemony of Britain (Lord Clive) and France (Dupleix) for the colonization of India. The convent is still used by the rich boys and girls of India and Lucknow. We would have stayed longer in that historical city, but we had already booked our tickets for Agra in Germany. We did not travel directly to Agra, but got off at Tundra Station, as it took much less time to reach Agra from there by taxi. We stayed at the hotel Wyndham, in the outskirt of Agra city. Dina enjoyed the surroundings of the hotel with its architecture and blooming pathways, spacious gardens, services, and swimming pools. Tara showed her the Taj Mahal, the Red Fort, and other important sights. Maria and I went with them to the Itimadud Daula Mausoleum, built by Nur Jehan in remembrance of his father. She was a Persian and was the beloved wife of the Mughal Emperor Jehangir (1569–1627). Many construction aspects of this mausoleum had been integrated in the Taj Mahal. From this place, we went to visit the Garden of Babur, he was the founder of the Mughal Empire (1526--1530) in India, descended on his father's side from Tamerlane and on his mother`s side from Chingiz Khan, the Garden of Babur possessed several plants from his birthplace von Turkestan. For our return to Delhi, we used for the first time the Jamuna Express Ways (Highway) from Agra to Delhi, we used this route, as it was newly constructed and shortened the journey to 165 km instead of 218 km and took only three hours of drive to Delhi, we stayed again in the hotel Royal Plaza, near Connaught Place. Tara knew Delhi well to show her daughter the historical and shopping places. I must tell you now the story of a marriage ceremony in our hotel. Most of the ceremonies of the rich in India take place in luxury hotels. When seeing the wedding fanfare, Dina became tempted to see it from close. Although, I was not invited to this, I proposed her to come with me. I told Dina that to attend a ceremony like that you needed to appear decent in decent clothing and look. After some hesitation, she joined me to the banqueting hall, where a lot of guests were enjoying their talks, drinks, food, and light music. A waiter told me the name of the father/uncle of the bridegroom, and I went straight to him saying: Mr. Chopra, I did not see you for a long time, I am just coming from abroad and do not dare to miss your invitation. Please let me introduce my granddaughter Dina to you. He was very pleased to hear that, welcomed us very warmly, and did not care to inquire about me in detail. I suppose, in the megacity of Delhi the most of the guests had hardly known each other, attend the ceremony as accidental acquaintances and trade partners of the hosts. He was just happy to have guests more from his side. I talked short with some guests, took some whisky, Dina some snacks and sweets, and then we parted from the scene silently. Thus, Dina had seen an Indian marriage ceremony and attended it and observed it was so simple to attend it. After this last exciting experience, we left Delhi.

2014 A year later, we flew to India again, this time with Tara and her two sons Luis and Adrian,12 and 9 years old, who had not been to India yet. Of course, we wanted to accompany them, as we had already done with our other grandchildren. Pranav waited for us with his Jaguar at Delhi Airport. Luis and Adrian were surprised to see a Jaguar in India and were glad to sit in it, but soon experienced, how dangerous and difficult it was to drive smoothly in the crowded city of Delhi, as more than 20 millions of people live and 25 % of the cars of India run alone in Delhi. We stayed again in the Hotel Royal Plaza. Because of my advanced age, I spent most of the time in our hotel, where my relatives and friends came to visit. Maria accompanied Tara, and her children most of the time in sightseeing and marketing places in Delhi, such as the Janpat, the emporiums, and the museums. Once Sharma came with his daughter Mona and her little son, who had arrived from Germany to meet her father in Noida, and visited us in the hotel. We had not seen them before, so we invited them with Sharma for dinner in our hotel. Luis, Adrian, and Sharman's grandson Shantanu spoke German with each other and went to the swimming pool of the hotel. Pranav's sister Parul, also came with her son to meet us. On the next day, we went with Luis and Adrian to the National Science Center, called Dream Castle. It is one of the biggest in Asia; Luis and Adrian were fascinated for hours in visiting it. At last, we took the children to Qutub Minar, Delhi's landmark. As planned, we left Delhi for Mussoorie, 300 km away. Tara had not been there before. The travel was smooth and save, except that the driver opened his door very often to spit out the red juice of betel (paan). Adrian felt sick and vomited a bit, as he was not accustomed to a long car trip on a bumping road. Soon we reached the hotel Claridge, formerly the residence of a British family, standing alone on a mountain of 2,400 m. This residence offered breakfast and dinner, so we did not have to go down to the mall to look for an afternoon meal, some ten to 12 km. During the day, we used the hotel's taxi service. Maria and Tara told me about their visits to the mall, to Gandhi Chowk, to convents, churches and to Gun Hill, where a rusty canon from British times could be seen. Maria showed Tara and the children her beloved Camel Back Road and took a walk with them there. We had already decided in Germany to go to from Mussoorie to Chandigarh, as it is not far from Mussoorie, only 206 km, the place offers a mild climate, is very clean and has interesting spots for the children. Having rested and had fun in Mussoorie for five days, we hired a car to go to Chandigarh. The road to Chandigarh was in good condition, and we reached our hotel, the hotel Taj, in sector 17 timely. Chandigarh is the richest city of India, with the highest per capita income and the highest number of expensive cars in India. The people of Punjab are know for their industrious lifes in India and abroad. We, the grown-ups, had already been in Chandigarh before. Tara and Maria went with the children to the Le Corbusier Planning Office, Rock Garden, Rose Garden, Sukhna Lake, and the shopping Center Sector 17. Once again, I met my old friend Puri in the Taj Hotel, but could not meet his wife, as she was suffering from an illness. Instead of taking the Shatabdi express, we booked a flight back to Delhi in an hour only. As the end of the children's school holidays was coming closer, our friend Sharma offered his car for a quick day trip to Agra via the Jamuna Express Highways. We showed the Taj Mahal to the children, and this was the last place of our visit to India.It was a Sunday, and the Taj was full of Indian visitors. By that time, the Indians had more money and the government brought the school children there at low cost of travel and stay. But the entry tickets for Europeans were still very expensive. Tara, Luis, and Adrian went to visit the Taj, while Maria and I sat and rested in the adjacent garden. While sitting there, I remembered of my visit with Jussi of the Humayun (1508–1556) Mausoleum in Delhi. Humayun had been Barbur's son, who had been the second Moghul Emperor (1526–1556). The Taj Mahal is a later construction based on this model. In a room of this mausoleum, the last Emperor of the Moghul Empire, Bahadur Shah Zafar (1775–1862) was arrested by the British in the mutiny of 1857 and brought in prison to Rangoon, where he died too. The entry ticket to see the Humayun Tomb had at that time been 500 rupees (Rs.) for a European visitor, but for an Indian, only Rs. 10. I declared myself and Jussi as Indians to save the amount of Rs. 980 Altogether, a sum high enough to get a very good meal in Delhi for both of us. The clerk at the counter looked at us and said to me: Sir, you look like an Indian, but the boy does not. So I felt much ashamed of my behavior and paid the entry fee of Rs. 500 for Jussi. We remained outside of the Taj, as we had been there several times there before. After the children had sufficiently seen of the Taj, we went to a restaurant Pizza Hut, which is situated near the hotel Amar. This place reminded us of our stay in this hotel and of our meals in the Pizza Hut together with Ina and her daughters Lilia and Matilda in 2011. After coming back to Delhi, Sharma invited us to a farewell meal in the restaurant of hotel Taj in Delhi on the next day. It was our last trip with our grandchildren to India.

2016 For the last time, we traveled to India together with Tara. This time too, we booked our tickets and hotels also in advance in Germany. Pranav wanted us very much to stay with him in his house in Greater Kailash. His father Vijay, his grandfather Chandu Lal and his grandson Pranav had very often stayed with us in Bremen. Once Pranav's grandmother also stayed with us. We never heard of her name as it is not usual to speak the name of an old person in India. Therefore, we stayed with him in his new Italian-style house that offered enough room for us. Tara enjoyed the company of his modern wife. She was much different from her older from her family members and even her husband Pranav. Rich boys and girls of Delhi have now greatly adopted the American way of life. After a stay of some days with them, we flew to Jaipur. Long ago on our first trip in 1974 to India, we had visited Jaipur with our two daughters Tara and Ina. Unfortunately, on the day of our flight to Jaipur 2016, Maria and Tara were suffering from stomach troubles. However, after arrival in Jaipur they recovered well in our hotel, which we had booked for the first time with TUI in Bremen. In between Jaipur (capital of the state) had changed a lot. We observed a lot of Indian tourists and Europeans coming as flat rate visitors from Delhi via Agra to Jaipur. We saw the Palace, the Hawa Mahal, and Jantar Mantar, which is known for its astronomical position and its stone sundial. Never before had we seen the massive Amer Fort on the hill of Aravelli, 11 km away from the city, built of marble and red stone by Raja Man Singh (1589 and 1614). Because of the enormous number of visitors arriving there on buses, it became extremely difficult to enter the Fort. After waiting in the long queue, we finally managed to see the Diwan e Khaas (special house of audience), the Diwan e Aam (hall for the commons), and the Sheesh Mahal (Mirror Palace). On the whole, the Fort was in dilapidated condition, the pavement, the outdoors and the stairs were in decay. Somebody told us that enough money for its maintenance came from internal and external sources, but that was pocketed by the bureaucrats. OrignaIly, we had planned to fly together from Jaipur to Patna to see my sister Gurya. But due to measures of health precautions, Maria and Tara canceled their travel to Patna and flew till Delhi only, whereas I flew to Patna alone. This was my last visit to Gurya, as very shortly after our meeting with her in Patna, she died. After a stay of two days in Patna, I flew to

Delhi to join Maria and Tara. In Delhi, we lived in the hotel Metropolitan & Spa, near the largest business and shopping centers of Connaught Place and Karol Bagh of Delhi. Tara had to join her medical services in Aachen soon, so she left us in Delhi. Maria and I, being pensioners, could stay longer and planned a holiday again in Chandigarh. Our friend Sharma wanted to join us, but because he got ill, he could not accompany us. However, he provided us with enough aqua pure, fruit, and wine for our stay in Chandigarh, where we had already been to relax in its green and calm ambiance three times. On our return from Chandigarh, Sharma was waiting for us to pick us up from the station in New Delhi. Just a few words about Sharma: He had learned photography in Köln and made several documentaries in India for America and Deutsche Welle in Köln. He became close to German culture and liked its food, drink, and music. He had lived with his German wife and his daughter Mona in the Defence Colony of Delhi for some time. He went to Gurgaon, 15 km away to buy cheese, sausages, and wines at a German shop for his German guests, which he served on German opera music. It was the last time that we saw him, the friend of our entire family.

Epilogue

On my grandchild Luis's request, I began to compose my biography in the city of Columbia, Missouri (USA), in 2017 where I was spending some time with my wife Maria to see Carl, my youngest grandson, the newly born son of my son Jussi, who is now working there as a surgeon. I started with a glimpse of my early life in Shakra, my college studies in Mumbai, my work in Qatar, my adventurous coming to Germany, my studies, my work, my marriage to a German, becoming a German citizen, which gave me reasons for adopting this country as my second homeland. However, I have always kept in contact with my roots in India, and as soon as I began to earn money, I went there, taking my wife, my children, and even my grandchildren there to show them my family, my kin, my village and my friends, and visited the places of interest in India since 1974. In this span of 42 years, the world changed a lot, also India. Much before Christ, many poly-ethics confessions of the world emerged in the soil of this subcontinent India with its fascinating morals and rules, the invaders and migrants of mono-ethic beliefs came too in large numbers from all corners of the East and Wes in search of the fertile lands of Indus, Ganges and Jamuna, two waters (do-aab) and Punjab (five waters: Beas, Chinab, Jhelum, Ravi, and Sutlej, all tributary of Indus) and for the colonial trade of the fabulous spices. They settled, adjusted, and integrated with the people of India, developed an unparallel legendary cosmopolitan culture, a unique society, "unity in diversity", as Jawaharlal Nehru (1889-1964), the first Prime Minister of independent India, wrote 1946 in his book "Discovery of India". The old Indian elite of India does not exist anymore today, the newly rich and the modern bureaucrats saw in the old Indian culture and tradition the roots of their backwardness and the causes of domination by the west, and imitated die Western way of life, as Rana Das Gupta observed in his book of "Capital. The Eruption of Delhi" (2014).

Thus, the old cultural heritage was doomed to decay and die. The epic tales (alha rudel), the Ram Sita stories (Ram Lila kahani), the wander theatres (natak, natangi), the puppet shows (kath putli tamasha), the wrestling art (kushti akhara), the snake charmer with flute (sapera with bansuri), the wedding ceremony of monkeys (bander ki biah/lagan), the reciting of Urdu songs (ghazals), mushara and qawwali for the masses with harmonium and tabla in maidans and dargahs (grave yards) of sufis, etc. are rarely seen in India today. Even the classical dances of India are fading away. Thus, the story of my travels tells about the bygone days and the buried culture of the Indian people. It is narrated in my own words from my dim memories, and intended for my children and grandchildren, who accompanied me lovingly to India. The story is also told for the coming generations of my root (gharana).

Kaifi, Columbia/Bremen 2019

Jussi, Maria with Carl and me in Columbia

Pictures of our travels to India

1974

Maria with Tara and Ina – all dressed in saris

My brother Haseeb (left), Tara (right), Ina (left), I (middle)

My grandmother (Nani)

1978

Tara (right), Ina (left), me with Jussi (arm), my uncle with his wife

We and my sister Gurya's family in Patna

My sister Tara and her family in Damla

Tara and Ina with cousins in Shakra

1997

My mother with her daughter Gurya in Patna

2008

Tara with a calf in Rishikesh between the Ganges and Ashrams

2011

Prakash and I in Hamburg

Lilia with me, Maria and the relatives in Shakra

Lilia and Matilda in Red Fort Agra, behind the Taj Mahal (from this corner of Red Fort Shah Jahan saw the Taj Mahal until his death)

Lilia, Maria, Ina and Matilda at Gupta's house in Delhi

2013

Maria (left) with Tara, Dina (right) and I in Rampur
before the Reza Library

Tara and Luis in Mussoorie

Maria (left), Sharma and I in the Taj Restaurant in Delhi

Luis (right) and Adrian in front of the Taj Mahal in Agra

Maria at Gupta's in Delhi

1974 and 2011

House in the village Skakra (North Bihar)

My biography. With a glimpse of the past culture in India

Dear Luis,

To have an interest in the roots of one's family and to ask one's grandfather about it is, of course, natural. I will tell you about my family and land, as far as I remember. I was born in the family of my maternal grandfather in the village of Shakra Faridpur, Post Office Dholi, District Muzaffarpur, Province Bihar, India. In those days, there did not exist anything like a registry office or an identity card in that part of the world. The inhabitants of a place knew each other. They were born there and died there and lived on their own. When the British occupied India, they introduced the system of birth registration, but only by admission to a British high school. So, at my admission to high school, I had to give my birth date on 12.12.1933, as said by my parent. They remembered, that I was born just before the greatest earthquake of Bihar/Nepal (8,4 of the scale) in January 1934; it was told to me that I was brought to a British Hospital in Muzaffarpur (District town) just after my birth which was some 18/20 km away from my village because I needed to be kept in an incubator for breathing. As my mother did not have enough milk, I was breastfed by a poor neighbor woman who had a small baby. As long this woman, my second mother (Ma) lived, she remained very much respected in my family and bestowed with presents. The house shown in "Our travels with our children to India" was built in 1934, shortly after my birth and the earthquake.

It was narrated that my paternal forefathers came to North Bihar, named it as Hamid Sarai. They were given a land gift (jagirdari) by the Moghul Emperor Akbar the Great in the

17th century. My grandfather Chaudhury Maulana Abdul Wahab was not only a big landowner (zamindar), but also an educated man who founded a very well- known Islamic theological learning institution in India which still exists today under the name of "Darum Uloom Ahmadia in the town of Laheriasarai/Darbhanga" of Bihar. He was also a nationalist and freedom fighter and served imprisonment with Rajendra Prasad, the first president (1950–1962) of India. At his birthplace in Bilaspur, a monument is erected in the memory of my grandfather. A picture of it is hanging in my room in Bremen. My father Abdul Mannan Qasmi was sent to "Jamia Millia Islamia College Delhi" for higher education. One of the founders of this college was Dr. Zakir Hussain, the third President (1967-1969) of India. My father remained in close contact with him till his death. After the education in Delhi, my father decided to live in Bombay (now Mumbai). He became a communist, engaged in a communist ship trade union, and worked for the Urdu newspapers of Mumbai.

My maternal grandfather, Abul Hasan from Shakra, was not so well-situated from his parental side, but was an entrepreneur, made his fortune by founding a hide & skin factory in Calcutta (now Kolkata). He took some skin workers (chamars, the untouchables) from Shakra to Kolkata, cleaned and refined his hide and skin into fine products, sold his products to the British traders for the manufacturing of leather goods. He earned enough through it, bought lands in Shakra, and became a landowner (zamindar). In my childhood, I went to Kolkata with my grandmother (Nani). She took me to a cinema house there, where she had also been for the first time in her life. At the outbreak of a fire in the film, she thought it to be real and wanted to run out of the cinema. She only had one son Yussuf, who died suddenly at an early age. So, she adopted me.

I remember little from my childhood. I suppose, at the age of six or seven, I became seriously ill for several weeks. The indigenous physicians (hakim, vaid) diagnosed a black fever (kala azaar). In accordance with Indian prescriptions, I was not allowed to eat anything at all. During my illness, I wished above all to eat grapes, which I had never tasted before. I saw grapes for the first time in my life from England in a fruit shop of Muzaffarpur, wrapped in cotton pieces and preserved in a small wooden box. I heard my grandmother asking our land administrator (munshi) to go to buy some grapes in the city of Muzaffarpur and saying: he must get some grapes for him, one does not know, how long he is going to live. Thus, I got my long-desired grapes.

As a young boy, I liked to visit one of my paternal aunts in the village of Damla. This village is situated near Champaran, where the British had indigo plantations and Gandhi started 1917 his satyagraha. My aunty family had two elephants as working animals for their fields. I sometimes went to her with a friend of mine. One of her elephants waited for us with a rider (mahwat) at the station of Kamtaul, some 12 km away from Damla. I remember the elephant crossing the river Bhagmati, drinking water and spraying it out of its trunk all over us sitting on its back on a seat (howda). That was the reason why I always arrived at my aunty wet with a shy feeling of embarrassment. According to the instruction of my mother, I ate there very little of sweet dishes with butter, milk, and sugar, in order to pretend, that we had enough of such delightful food in Shakra. On my return, I always received a good amount of money from her, more than anyone gave me. With this money, I could visit the cinema several times and buy sweets (mithai, jelebi, gulab jamun, rasugulla). That reminds me of my many poor relatives. Fortunately, we had enough mango trees. But we could not consume or sell them, due to the lack of purchasing power of the people. Therefore my grandmother sent me to her poor relatives with mangoes to them. A servant, usually batahia (deaf and dumb), carried a basket of 20 to 25 mangoes on head to a far village on a train or foot. I accompanied her all the way, so they were not taken away from her/his by strangers.

No doubt, my village was better developed than others. It had a middle and high school with English teaching, a post office (daak ghar), a police station (thana), a registry office (kacheri), a dispensary (small hospital) with a medicine mixer in a glass (compounder) and a railway station, named Dholi. All that existed because of the presence of a British family of Danbys, who had a farm in Dholi on the bank of the Gandak river, a tributary of the Ganges, near to Shakra. Without a British education and a railway line in my village, I would perhaps never have been able to get so far. 1960 was Danby's farm converted into the second biggest agricultural college (Tirhut Agricultural College) of India. Your grandmother Maria visited 1978 this college with me, Tara and Ina. There we found a lot of neem trees used for tooth-brushing and antiseptic purposes.

Being a schoolboy, you will be glad to know how I passed my days in my village. After school hours, I played catching and throwing a wooden stick (kabaddi), playing marbles (goli khel), kite flying, cutting off other kites (guddi), hiding (chupna) and climbing (chaherna) the trees of fruits, etc. I went to the bazaar and the village market (haat) to buy things for the family. When I heard the train coming to the station Dholi, some 200 m away from our house, I ran to the station to see the activities on the platform, passengers of the train. Above all, I was very interested in seeing the coal engine, the loading of coal and filling of its water tank, black face of the engine staff, the driver and guard tokens and whistles to start and the hectic of station employees in loose British uniforms. During those days most of the Railway stuff in rank came from Bengal, where the Bristh first arrived. The Bengalis were educated to be a "class of persons, Indian in blood and colour but English in taste, in opinions, in morals and intellect" as Thomas Macaulay, the governer of Agra recommended in 1935.

I remember well the festivals, such as Dasserah, Diwali, Durga Puja, Holi, Id, und Muharram, which were celebrated by different communities for days. That often reminds me of wedding ceremonies, which lasted at least for two days. The hundreds of bridegroom guests coming to the house of the bride on foot, on bullock carts, donkeys, ponys, horses, and elephants with musical instruments like drums (dholak) tabla), horns, trumpets, sarangi (string instrument), and the bridegroom always sitting on a decorated horse with garlands with a gorgeous costume. At such ceremonies, it was interesting to see the dancing woman (nachwali), singers, acrobats, and even man of fart (padwala), who farted on order and gave a few extra as a gift. I went to see the cooking for the hundreds of persons and inside the tent (shamiana) to witness the mass feeding of the guests (barati), where often quarrel arose on grounds of the quality and quantity of food, drink and sleeping arrangements. I loved to see the gifts (saman, jahez, tilak) presented to the married couple. It was always heartbreaking for me to hear the weeping of the villagers and parents at the departure of the bride (bidai, rukhsati) to the family of the bridegroom. The reason for such sorrow was obvious, as sometimes the poor bride never came back to her parents.

On this occasion, I think of our baldachin (dauli, palki), which was used my grandmother and mother to attend a ceremony of near relatives. Your grandmother Maria saw 1974 this palki in our courtyad, but on her second visit in 1978 it was no more there. My mother told us that it had been burnt for our earthen cooker (chula) and due to the lack of its carriers (kumhar) , as they had all migrated to Punjab or somewhere to work as labourers. Of course, such ceremonies were not always, but our days were full of other excitements, as the sudden appearance of a snake charmer (sapera), a dancing beer (bhalu) to blow the buttock of a child to make him thick, the marriage of monkeys (bander ki biah), coming of a mascular man (pahelwan) for wrestling in a field (akhara) of the village, a natangi (village theater), a jogi/sanyasi/sadhu/fakir with ascetic look and mystic songs on the way to a pilgrimage.

During the days of my childhood, India was absolutely an agrarian society. After the harvest, the traveling theatres (natak, nautangi) went from village to village. The actors who were only men played always the role of a female. They played from the epic stories of Mahabharata and Ramayana and from the tales of thousand and a night, Ali Baba and the forty thieves, Thief of Baghdad, the love story of Laila Majnun, Heer und Rangha, etc.

In great excitement, I waited for the arrival of the gypsy (banjara, khana-badosh). They usually stayed in our field of mangoes and lichis. The men worked as kettle menders, knife grinders, dealers of second-hand utensils, and their women sold mostly handmade ornaments and embroidery and saw hands as fortune-tellers for the women. During their stay, the villagers remained alert and awake, as they were afraid of becoming victims of the gypsy.

I remember well some of the events of my school days. My grandmother (Nani) woke me before the break of dawn and came with an earthen kerosene lamp (dibia): She used to say: “Dawn is the best time to learn. When you read, concentrate like a heron (bagula) to catch a fish and repeat loud like a crow (kawua), so instructs a Guru (teacher) to his chela (disciple).” Those times, a few of the schoolboys came to me to learn, as they could not afford a lamp at their homes. These boys passed the matriculation examination with me and got good employments somewhere.

Regarding education in those time it was easy to have a simple job in British services of railways, coat, police, post, etc., if one has only read the “English First Book” which contained only simpel reading and writing. So I remember a postman (peon) who came to deliver post and money order in our village. He came first to our house and was always offered by my grandmother the waterpipe (huqqa), betel (paan) and tea with milk and sugar. He enjoyed it all and read out the interesting postcards in Hindi or Urdu (chitthi, khat) of other recipients.

I must also tell you that my family had a slim dog from Nepal, called Jelly. Jelly brought for me in the afternoon a meal to my high school, tied around his neck. He waited patiently for me to come out of the class and to take the empty plates back to my house. When I left silently in the evening to go to Muzaffarpur to see a film in a cinema, Jelly followed me to the station Dholi. He waited for me at the railway station in the arrival hours of my train and barked in pleasure so much, that everyone in my house woke up. My grandmother and mother grumbled loudly at me and warned me in strict words to visit the cinema anymore. Since then, I have always liked so much the company of a dog, although I never had a dog in Germany. I soon became very familiar with Rexi, the dog of your great grandmother in Rehbach, near Köln. The dog of your uncle Jussi in Columbia (USA), also named Rexi, followed me everywhere when I stayed with him there.

Some events remained always in my mind. A teacher of my high school in Shakra, Anugra Singh, whose home was some 50 km away from our school, lived in our house and taught me algebra and geometry. He was a pure vegetarian, cooked his food himself, and washed his dishes. Some evenings we went to the cinema in Muzaffarpur together. On the way, he told me of his parents, wife, and children. He wished to live with his family in his native place, but he could not find a teaching job there. I still remember his simplicity, sadness, and longings after his home. It belongs to my story that I grew up in a big Indian family with disabled and homeless persons. They were nameless and called according to their fates and physical conditions as lame (lengra), one eyed (kana), deaf (gungra), batahia (deaf and dumb), dwarf (bhutta), widow (bewa, musmat), parentless (yatim), etc. We lived together with them, as everyone did some essential work in the family. Although our elder relatives had birth names which were never spoken out. We named our first uncle/aunt from fatherside as bara chacha/ bara chachi, the middle one as majhla chacha/majhili chachli and the last one chota chacha/choti chachi. This kind of denomation with respect was used throughout India.

There existed also some old customs in our society, which were not so favorable for a destitute kin. When such a person visited us and lived in our family for some days, he was served rye bread (marua ki roti) and eggplant (baigan) to eat and tea without milk and sugar as a sign for an unwanted guest. This was also very interesting for Dr. Viorel Roman from the University of Bremen to see in Shakra 1972 of the harvest time, the washerman (dhobi), the haircutter (nai, hajam), the cobbler (chamar), the toilet cleaner (bhangi, mehter) and the carcass remover (dom), gravedigger (nunia) before our farms to collect their share of grains for their yearly services. This system of barter had existed for centuries as a pillar of Indian society, as even Karl Max mentioned this in his different publications on India since 1853. With the abolition of zamindari and the barter system eradicated the rural structure of India.

I remember from the days of my childhood the coming of

the Kabuliwala, then so called Pashtu/Khan from Afghanistan. They came to our villages to sell the handmade woollen blankets (kambal) and the spice named devil's dung (hing, Latin: asafoetida), used very fondly in the lentils (daals) of Indians. They sold these products in advance on high interest rates (suudh). When the customer became unable to pay the due, I heard often the Kabuliwala abusing and threatening the debtor in their language of Pashtu (a branch language of Sanskrit) which was very interesting to me and others to hear. It was told to us that the Kabuliwalas using trains in India kept deliberately the bags of devil dung in their compartment and its smell kept even the ticket controller away. The partition of the Subcontinent in 1947 and the creation of boundaries between India, Pakistan and Afghanistan let abandon such century old human and trade movements of people.

Now I live in a wealthy western society, but my mind still goes back to the bygone days. I come from the delta of Ganges in "Bihar. The heart of India" as described by John Houlton in his book written in 1949. Much before Christ the Hinduism, Buddhism and Jainism was born here and the imperiums of Lichchavi, Magadha and Maurya existed in this delta of Bihar. This part is known too for its Himalayan Monsoon (Arabic Mausam, the "direction of the wind) and for havoc of floods (barh, sailab) to bring the destruction of lives, harvests, starvation and diseases, displacing to millions of people in search of living in the cities of India and abroad.

So, I left my birthplace too. Our ancestral land began to be divided among shareholders. After the end of my matriculation 1948, I had to think about the future of my life. I remained as a manly representative of my family in my village for four years. My father had never felt attached to the countryside and its people and had gone long ago to Mumbai. He asked me to come to Mumbai to study in a modern college. Luckily, I met a school companion who was looking for better work opportunities in Mumbai. I got a chance to have a travel partner for a distance of some 2,000 km. The journey took more than three days and two nights. For hours we waited at stops to get coal or water, or for the repair of the locomotive and for the crossing of the trains, as the lines were small (choti) and single-track. Sometimes we crossed a bridge on foot because it was being repaired, damaged, and flooded. By crossing a river, we heard the calling of the passengers shouting, long live mother Ganges (Ganga mata ki jai). In spite of all these happenings, we enjoyed the coming and going of passengers in varied clothes with heavy goods on the head and small animals in hands. We looked at the hawkers (wallas) with chai, pakoras, samosas, puris, roti, paan, cigarettes, etc. We heard the epic stories, the songs of Tulsidas and Kabir, sung by sadhus, fakirs, blind beggars, and I saw people and things, which I had never seen before: the basins, the valleys, the arid lands, jungles, the hilly ranges of Vindayachal and the plateau of Deccan, passing through our eyes. All these scenes kept us busy throughout our journey. Tired, malnourished, dirty, our hair black with soot, we finally reached Mumbai, where my father picked us up from the famous Victoria Terminal. It was perhaps there where I first realized that my rural life in Bihar had come to an end.

In Mumbai, I studied in Wilson College from 1952 to 1956. It was an old Irish missionary college situated at Chowpatty on the Arabian Sea. During my studies, I stayed for some time with my family members in the area of Byculla and Haji Ali in Worli at the Arabian Sea. I lived most of the time alone in different parts of the city and earned some money by giving extra tuition in English to the children. During our stays in Mumbai in 1974 and 1978, your grandmother Maria met a few of my old friends there. After I had graduated with a bachelor's degree in economics in 1956, my father suggested to continue my studies of Master of Arts (M.A.). But his health condition was deteriorating, and I wished to stand on my own feet. Therefore I asked him to help me find a job. At that time, it was very difficult to get a job in India without recommendations and connections. Fortunately, my father had a very prominent friend in Mumbai, Jahya Jasdanwala, who was an industrialist and an agent of British Petroleum in India. Through this connection, I got employment for three years as a bookkeeper at the Petroleum Company of Qatar. In Qatar, I worked mostly in the central administration of the company and at its drill locations in the desert, where petroleum had not been found yet. My duty was to maintain a register of presence and absence list of the drilling employees for the payment of wages. The workers were mostly desert dwellers (baddus) and Asians. I lived in a tent, got good food and tea with British cakes in a tin box and was satisfied with living there. Twice a year, I was flown by helicopter with other employees to Manama, the capital of Bahrain, 470 km, to spend a holiday of two days there. During my employment, I sometimes saw sheiks visiting our camp on a donkey. The British chief gave us instructions to bow down before the sheiks. The British hoped to find petroleum there and acted very friendly towards the rulers of the desert. At the end of my three-year contract in 1959, I had to go back to India. My father advised me not to come back to India. He thought of my marriage, which was being prepared by my family members for the good presents (jahez) and money (tilak). He asked me to continue my studies in England and sent me a recommendation letter of his friend for the Indian Embassy in London. I still have this letter with me. Before my departure, I had the names of the countries on my travel route entered by the Indian Consul in Muscat (Oman). I left the port of Doha in Qatar on a ship named Daressa and reached Basra in 3 days. After a night's stay at the Indian consul, I left Basra by bus to go to Baghdad. I assume I traveled the whole night in a very crowded bus. I remained in Baghdad for a couple of days to buy a ticket for the legendary train of Orient Express. I do not remember the names of the countries and places of my stops and stays. I do remember only a few cities, such as Basra, Baghdad, Aleppo, Istanbul, Salanoki, Belgrad, Zagreb, and the hilly areas of Switzerland and Germany. My baggage consisted of only one big handmade leather trunk with my clothes, a Walflex camera, a Remington shaving machine, gifts from friends in Qatar. I carried all cash, e.g., dinars, and my traveler cheques in my pocket, even at night. Your grandmother Maria is still preserving my pictures of my mates from Qatar, camera, and trunk from Mumbai. I think it took me two weeks to reach Germany. I still remember a few events. At the time I was in Basra, the British had been displaced for the first time by a local military power of Iraq. The local officer on the ship did not accept my entry permit for British Iraq, and I was detained on the ship to be sent back to Doha the next day. After the intervention of the Indian and the British Consulate, I was allowed to enter Iraq and continue my journey. During my stay in Baghdad, I slept on a roof of an old Sarai on the banks of the river Tigris. On one of the borders of Turkey, the passengers were controlled. I had to open my trunk, in which the controller saw my British atlas. There he saw Constantinople as the capital of Turkey. He became furious reading this old name and said to me loudly: It is called now Istanbul and not Constantinople, and scratched out the word Constantinople with his pencil. In Belgrad, I was held up by a customs officer on 30.08.1959 when he saw my traveler checks worth 360 pounds sterling. He could not understand that an Indian should have so much money with him. After talks with his superior officer, he wrote the amount on my checks in my passport and then allowed me to travel further. Here, I must tell you that none of my belongings were stolen on the ship, bus, Orient Express, or somewhere else. I think people in those days were more honest and kind to foreigners. Only once, a launderer did not appear in Belgrad to give me back my two silk shirts, which I was carrying as a costly present of a good friend of mine from Doha.

As I said earlier, my original intention had been to go to London. But during my journey on the Orient Express, I met a boy of my own age from Iraq who was traveling to Germany. He talked about Germany in a very positive way in regard of admission, education, scholarships, and earning in that country. He told me that Germans were not racists anymore but friendly to people of color. He warned me of the British. They were arrogant and regarded the people of their former colonies as inferior. He made me so scared and uncertain about Great Britain that I changed my mind to go there. Following his advice, I stopped in Bonn, the capital of West Germany, in September 1959. I could not believe Bonn was the capital l of Germany. I saw a devastated city with many disabled people. I lived for a few days in a fully war-damaged hotel, opposite of the Bonn railway station. I went to the cultural attaché of the Indian Embassy in Bonn for instructions. Having a Bachelor of Art in Economy (B. A.), I was recommended by him to the University of Köln, which was then the best-known university for economic studies in Germany. I went to a Commerz Bank in Bonn to change my cheque to Deutsche Mark (DM). The bank clerk looked at me surprised, noted the data of my passport and travel documents and told me it would take at least 3 weeks to cash the checks. In those days, it took a lot of time to control and verify the validity of such papers. Then I left for Köln on the small train of Rhine shore (Rheinuferbahn). At the information center of Köln, I had been given addresses of hostels for students, and I received a room in an Evangelic student hostel in Bachemer Street. After three weeks, I went to Bonn to ask the bank for my money. To my great disappointment, the employee told me that my cheques had still not been confirmed for payment and that I had to wait for it some more time. I became upset, as I did not have sufficient money to buy a return ticket for Köln. It was getting late, and I did not know anybody to borrow the needed amount. Thus, I decided to go back to Köln on foot. I walked along the railway line of the Rheinuferbahn from Bonn to Köln, some 25 km. I reached my hostel thirsty, hungry and tired in the middle of the night. Ultimately, after some two weeks, I received the amount of DM 4,100 at an exchange rate of 1 pound = DM 14,60, which was somewhere enough for me to study for a year. Then my real life started in Köln. I lived in the city, met friends, ate in the University canteen, and took temporary jobs at the Student Employment Office (Studentenschnelldienst) in order to save my money from Qatar. I was admitted to the faculty of Business Economy (Betriebswirtschaft) by the middle of 1960. An episode comes to my mind which I would like to tell you. In those days, foreign students were invited for Christmas by German families and institutions. On that occasion, I was invited by my Evangelic hostel. A Palestinian friend of mine from Bethlehem showed his interest in attending the ceremony in my hostel. He did not like his former host's invitation, as he feared to play the role of a Moor king under a Christmas tree again.

During a holiday in 1961, I got a job through the job mediation center for University students in Köln (Schnellstudentendienst) in the central department of curtains of Kaufhof in Köln. The chief of this department was Lange. He admired me after having heard the story of my life and made me work as supervisor of this department, where mostly students worked. In this department of curtains, I met your grandmother, with whom I live together till today. In the same period, I came to know Prof. Gerhard Weiser of the faculty of Social Politics of the University of Köln. He was shocked to hear, that I had already spent nearly all my savings earned in Qatar and quickly arranged for me a scholarship of DM 250 from the Friedrich- Ebert-Stiftung in Bonn. Later I came to know that he was one of the significant people of this eminent Social- Democratic Foundation in Germany. Through the seminars of this foundation, I came to know much about the economic and political history of Germany. I met by chance Prof. Karl Newman, who had migrated to India in the days of Hitler and had come back to Köln. He gave me a part-time job in his library of politics for a monthly salary of DM 150. Apart from that, I earned some money in the Indian Hindi and economy departments of Deutsche Welle (Voice of Germany) as a writer on subjects of India and the Third World.

All these earnings enabled me to have a good life in Köln. I could afford a room with central heating in Dassel Street near to the university. For the first time in Köln, I had a common toilet near, and a bathroom. I could also cook my food in my room and had a new refrigerator and a new radio. All this looked like a sheer luxury for a foreign student. Some Indian, Asian, European students and even Prof. Neumann himself came to me to eat my Indian spicy food. At that time, there was no Indian restaurant or shop in Köln.

During my studies in Köln, I met many students from China, Egypt, Indonesia, Iran, Iraq, Pakistan, Latin America, and Indians from African countries, such as from Kenya, South Africa, and Uganda, who had to leave were some African states. Some of those students stayed in Germany forever. A few of them attended my 80th birthday in 2013 in the hotel Kölner Hof.

I passed my examination as Diplom-Kaufmann in 1966 and married in 1967 your grandmother Maria in Köln. After my graduation, I began to do research on a thesis entitled "Banking development and economic situation of India" by Prof. Hahn of the University of Köln. Unfortunately, the professor went on an exchange to his partner University of Kabul (Afghanistan). Therefore I was left alone with my work and did not know what to do. I needed a job to assist my newly founded family. Accidently, I met a university librarian, Dr. Solbach, in Köln, and she advised me to join the library services. Due to the foundation of several new Universities in Germany, economists were in high demand for University libraries. In 1968, I became a trainee (Referendar) at the "Library Institute of the State of North-Rhine Westphalia Köln" (Bibliothekar Lehrinstitut des Landes Nordrhein-Westfalen in Köln). During my training as a librarian, your grandmother was doing the teacher training for Gymnasium in the city of Wuppertal at the same time. In 1968, I met there by accident the Iraqi from the Orient Express, who was now working as a salesman in the furniture department of the storehouse Kaufhof. At the end of my training 1971, I submitted an empirical work on the use of the University library of Köln by foreign students (Bibliotheksbenutzung von ausländischen Studenten in Köln). It was regarded as the first research work of its kind by a foreign Student and was published under the same headline in the journal of Association of Libraries of North-Rhine Westfalia. 22(3). 1971 (Mitteilungsblatt. Verband der Bibliotheken des Landes Nordrhein-Westfalen, Jahrgang 22(3). 1971). This work was also compiled in "Towards the Research on the use of Libraries. Saur Publication 1971" (Zur Benutzerforschung in Bibliotheken. Saur Verl. 1971). These publications helped me to get a job soon. I was employed as consultant (Referent) for the subject of economy in the newly founded University library of Hansa State of Bremen. After a year of working there, the Director of this University library Dr. Kluth recommended the State of Bremen to naturalize me. 1973 I was granted a German citizenship. Along with me, your mother Tara and your aunt Ina got automatically the German citizenship, which made our lives in Germany and traveling abroad much easier. My former training for higher jobs as a librarian in Germany and my naturalization made it possible for me to become a civil servant (Beamter) and 1973 a Bibliotheksrat. 1974 I was selected head for the Department of Economy and Law at the University library of Bremen. 1974 I was promoted to a higher position as Oberbibliotheksrat. I was perhaps the first foreigner by birth to become a civil servant in a high position in the State of Bremen.

I must tell you frankly that in the early phase of my marriage, I was seen with skepticism and suspicion by the family of your grandmother. But by that time, I became well accepted and integrated in the family. I remember with deep sorrow having carried a few members of this of your German grandfather, grandmother, your uncle to the graveyards.

I kept myself intellectually active in Germany. At the age of 56, I submitted my dissertation at the University of Oldenburg on "Social Economic Determinants of Health Service in India under the Colonial Structures". Fischer Verlag. Frankfurt /Main. 1991 (Sozio-ökonomische Determinant des indischen Gesundheitwesens unter kolonialer Strukturen), which was 1992 published in English by the same publisher.

For a couple of years, I was engaged as a lecturer (Lehrbeauftragter) of the University of Oldenburg on the subjects of Social Economic Problems of the Third World. Since long I am writing articles on migration, employment, and integration of Indians, Asian and Africans in Germany, which had been published in joint works, yearbooks and journals of Germany and outside, see my homepage "www. Indien-welt.weebly.com". I worked voluntarily for many years in academic associations of Germany, such as in "Evangelical Organization in Müllheim an der Ruhr" and in the Society of Asian and African Academics in Göttingen".

By composing my bibliography, I have deliberately avoided speaking of my troubles and hardship in Germany. In such hours, my family and friends had always stood by my side and I consoled myself with words: "Have patience, after the darkness comes the light".

Dear Luis, the story of your grandfather is one among those of innumerable migrants. Long ago, a physician in Bremen seeing my fractured rib, told me, that my forefathers had probably come from a part of the Urals/ Volga to India. The ancestors of your grandmother Nelles migrated from France to Germany. So, you are a product of both East and West. Your mother Tara and your aunty Ina were born in Köln, your uncle Jussi in Bremen. You and your sister Dina and your brother Adrian live in Aachen, Ina lives with her daughters Lilia and Matilda in Berlin and Jussi with his son Carl in Columbia, Missouri, in the USA. Who knows where our offspring will live and end up? I pray and wish for my children, grandchildren, and all of my descendants the best of luck.

Your grandfather, Dr. Dipl. Kfm. Abdul Khaliq Kaifi (Bibliotheksoberrata.D.), at the moment in Columbia,12.12.2018. translated from German into English in March 2021 in Bremen.

My Publications

Studenten aus Entwicklungsländern schätzen die Ausbildung auf deutschen Universitäten.In: Kölner Stadt-Rundschau. 28. Dezember 1962. S. 14/Nummer 300

Farbige unter Weißen. In: Vorwärts. Bad Godesberg. 27. März 1963. S. 15

Über 50 Beiträge des Autors über Entwicklungsländer sind von der „Deutschen Welle“ Köln zwischen 1967 und 1972 gesendet worden (s. Deutsche Welle Manuskripte)

Bremen kann einen neuen Anfang setzen. Universitäten bieten Ausländern zu wenig Hilfe.In: Weser-Kurier. 18. August 1971. S. 3

Bibliotheksbenutzung durch ausländische Studenten (Auszüge der Arbeit zur Prüfung für den höheren Dienst an wissenschaftlichen Bibliotheken der BRD 1971). In: Zur Benutzerforschung in Bibliotheken. Verlag Pullach. München 1972. S. 153-164 und In: Mitteilungsblatt. Verband der Bibliotheken des Landes Nordrhein-Westfalen. Neue Folge. Jg. 22 (3). 1971. S.190–197

Bestandsverzeichnis der Fachbibliographien Wirtschaftswissenschaften. Staats- und Universitätsbibliothek Bremen. 1975. S. 24

Literaturdokumentation wirtschaftswissenschaftlicher Projekte 1972-1975. Universität Bremen. 1975. S. 98

Studien- und Bibliothekshilfsmittel für die Studierenden der Wirtschaftswissenschaften an der Universität Bremen. 1976. S. 95

Verzeichnis multinationaler Konzerne im Weltwirtschaftssystem. Universität Bremen. 1978. S. 242

Literaturdokumentation wirtschaftswissenschaftlicher Projekte 1972–1980. Universität Bremen. 1980. S. 163

Großbanken im Weltwirtschaftssystem. Universität Bremen. 1980. S. 289

Sozio-ökonomische Determinanten des indischen Gesundheitswesens unter Berücksichtigungkolonialer Strukturen. Dissertation Universität Oldenburg. Frankfurt/M. 1990. S. 276

Socio-economic Determinants of Health Systems in India under the Aspect of Colonial Stuctures. Frankfurt/M. 1991. S. 284

Medizin, Gesellschaft und Gesundheitssysteme im afroasiatischen Raum. In: Traditionelles Wissen und Modernisierung. Hrsg. Afrikanisch-Asiatische Studentenförderung Göttingen. Jahrbuch 1991.Frankfurt/M. S. 192–205

Wasser als Bestimmungsfaktor der sakralen Macht und Despotie im Leben der Völker.In: Rundbrief. Jg. 7(2). Göttingen 1992. S. 25–28

Die Studenten aus der Dritten Welt in Deutschland gestern und heute. In: Afrika Asien Rundbrief.Jg.10(2). Göttingen 1995. S. 32–33

Migration und Migranten in Deutschland. In: Afrika Asien Rundbrief. Jg.15(4). Göttingen 2000.S.13-15

Migranten aus Afrika und Asien in Hamburg. In: Afrika Asien Rundbrief. Jg. 16 (1). Göttingen 2001. S. 13-21

NGOs und Berufschancen für AkademikerInnen in ihren Heimatländern (organisiert und geleitet).In: Afrika Asien Rundbrief. Jg. 16 (4). Göttingen 2001. S. 21-27

Afrikaner und Asiaten in Deutschland. In: Afrika Asien Rundbrief. Jg. 17(2). Göttingen. 2002.S. 16-17

Die Kasten und Klassen Indiens im Spannungsfeld des Machtanspruchs und der ökonomischen Entwicklung. In: Ökonomische Ethik in Afrika und Asien. Hrsg. Afrikanisch-Asiatische Studentenförderung.Jahrbuch 1995. Frankfurt/M. 1995. S. 176-191

Kasten- und Klassenstruktur Indiens. In: Wider den Geist. Festschrift zum 65. Geburtstag von

Prof. Dr. Ravasani. Hrsg. Andreas Lembeck. Universität Oldenburg 1996. S. 159-180

Diskussionsbeitrag. In: Meine Welt. Zeitschrift zur Forderung des Deutsch-Indischen Dialogs.Jg. 14(1). Köln 1997. S. 17-27

Beitrag des Südens zur technisch-naturwissenschaftlichen-Entwicklung des Nordens am Beispiel der Medizin. In: Globalisierung der Wissenschaft: Süden-Forschung im Norden. Hrsg. Afrikanisch-Asiatische Studentenförderung. Jahrbuch. 1997.Frankfurt/M. 1997. S. 125-136

Islam und andere Religionen. In: Meine Welt. Jg. 15(2). Köln 1998. S. 3

Ausländische Studenten in Deutschland. Hrsg. Afrikanisch-Asiatische Studentenförderung. Jahrbuch 1998. Frankfurt/M. 1998. S. 15–26

Inder in Deutschland. In: Meine Welt. Jg. 16(2). Köln 1999. S. 4–6

Migration und Migranten in Deutschland. In: Afrika Asien Rundbrief. Jg. 15(4). Göttingen 2000.S. 13–15

Zivilgesellschaft und Moslems in Indien. In: Die Entwicklung der Zivilgesellschaft in afro-asiatischen Ländern und Chancen der Reintegration nach dem Auslandsstudium. Hrsg. Afrikanisch- Asiatische Studentenförderung. Jahrbuch 2000. Frankfurt/M. 2000. S. 35–44

Migranten aus Afrika und Asien in Hamburg. In: Rundbrief. Jg. 16(1). Göttingen 2001. S. 13–21

NGOs und Berufschancen für AkademikerInnen in ihren Heimatländern. In: Afrika Asien Rundbrief. Jg. 16(4). Göttingen 2001. S. 21–28 (Tagung organisiert und geleitet von mir)

Mobilitätsstudien. Zur Attraktivität des Studienortes Deutschland in Asien. Hrsg. Deutscher Akademischer Austauschdienst (DAAD). Besprechung. In: Asien. Deutsche Zeitschrift für Politik, Wirtschaft und Kultur. Nr. 81(2001). Hamburg 2001. S. 130–131

Die Möglichkeiten und Chancen der Unanibehandlung im indischen Subkontinent. In: Twenty First Century Bangladesh. Ed. Gulam Abu Zakaria. Bangladesh Study and Development Centre. Wiehl. 2001. S. 75–82 (Erschienen in bengalischer Sprache)

Unani, The Graeco-Arab Medicine in India. In: Studies in History of Medicine & Science. Vol. XVIII. No. 2. New Series (2002). Delhi. S. 15–37

Afrkaner und Asiaten in Deutschland. In: Afrikaner und Asiaten in Deutschland-Multiplikatoren des Wissenschaftstransfers zwischen Süd und Nord. Hrsg. Afrikanisch-Asiatische Studentenförderung. Jahrbuch 2001. Frankfurt/M. 2001. S. 1–16

Moslems im demokratischen Indien-Gegenwart und Zukunft. In: Meine Welt. Jg. 19(1). Köln 2002.S. 4–7

Das Vermächtnis von HazratKhawajaMoinuddinChisti von Ajmer. In: Meine Welt. Jg.19(2). Köln 2002. S. 18

Unani, die griechisch-arabische Medizin in Indien. In: Meine Welt. Jg. 20(1). Köln 2003. S. 47–50

Sufis und Sufismus in Indien. In: Meine Welt. Jg. 20(2). Köln 2003. S. 44–50

Musik in Indien-Vergangenheit und Gegenwart. In: Meine Welt. Jg. 21(2). Köln 2004. S. 16–20

Tanz in Indien. In: Meine Welt. Jg. 22(1). Köln 2005. S. 40–45

Film in Indien und Bollywood. In: Meine Welt. Jg. 22(3). Köln 2005. S. 41–45

Malerei in Indien. In: Meine Welt. Jg. 24(1). Köln 2007. S. 36-39

Eine besondere Persönlichkeit. Zur Erinnerung an Frau Dr. Gosalia. In: Meine Welt. Jg.25(1). Köln 2008. S. 17-18

Gerhard Schweizer. Der unbekannte Islam. Stuttgart 2007. Besprechung. In: Meine Welt. Jg. 25(1). Köln 2008. S. 31-32

Architektur in Indien. In: Meine Welt. Jg. 25(2). Köln 2008. S. 62-68

Indien und China. Begegnungen auf der Seidenstrasse. In: Meine Welt. Jg. 27(1). Köln 2010.S. 42-45

Indische Diaspora in Afrika. In: Meine Welt. Jg. 28(2). Köln 2011. S. 51-58

Indische Emigranten in Europa und Nordamerika. In: Meine Welt. Jg.29(1). Köln 2012. S. 45-48

Die Kasten und Klassenstruktur Indiens im Umbruch. In: Meine Welt. Jg. 30(3). 2013/14. S. 45-50

Wasser als Instrument himmlischer und irdischer Macht in Indien, In: Meine Welt, 28.02.2014

For further Information, see indienwelt.weebly.com

www.ingramcontent.com/pod-product-compliance
Ingram Content Group UK Ltd.
Pitfield, Milton Keynes, MK11 3LW, UK
UKHW041844200726
13854UKWH00005BA/2057

9 783754 364451